Estimating Reading Ability

The following graded word lists may be used to estimate a student's reading grade level.

1. Ask the student to read each word in the list.

2. Keep count of the number of words the student reads from the list.

3. Estimate the student's ability to read materials at the same grade level as the grade level of the word list. Base your estimate upon:

23 or more   The student can probably read at this grade level without help.

18 - 22   The student can probably read at this grade level if given some help.

17 or less   The student can probably not read at this grade level even if given help.

1.	attic	13.	guide
2.	beneath	14.	hero
3.	bubble	15.	impatient
4.	cent	16.	knife
5	coast	17.	lookout
6.	cream	18.	merry
7.	decorate	19.	needle
8.	dozen	20.	package
9.	entrance	21.	pinch
10.	fever	22.	scrap
11.	footstep	23.	snuggle
12.	glove	24.	title
		25.	yarn

©1995 Kelley Wingate Publications, Inc.   CD-3710

Ready-To-Use Ideas and Activities

The activities in this book will help children master the basic skills necessary to become competent learners. Remember as you read through the activities listed below, as you go through this book, that all children learn at their own rate. Although repetition is important, it is critical that we never lose sight of the fact that it is equally important to build children's self-esteem and self-confidence if we want them to become successful learners as well as good citizens.

If you are working with a child at home, try to set up a quiet comfortable environment where you will work. Make it a special time to which you each look forward. Do only a few activities at a time. Try to end each session on a positive note, and remember that fostering self-esteem and self-confidence is also critical to the learning process.

Story Comprehension

During or after story discussion, there are two different types of questions that you can ask to ensure and enhance reading comprehension. The first type of question is a factual question. This type of question includes question words such as: who, what, when, where, and why. It can also include questions like How old is the character?, Where does the character live?, What time was it when....?, or any question that has a clear answer. The other type of question is an open-ended question. These questions will not have a clear answer. They are based on opinions about the story, not on facts. An open-ended question can be something like: Why do you think the character acted as he did?, How do you think the character felt about her actions or the actions of others?, What do you think the character will do next?, or What other ways could this story have ended?.

Flashcard ideas

The back of this book has removable flash cards that will be great for use for basic skill and enrichment activities. Pull the flash cards out and either cut them apart or, if you have access to a paper cutter, use that to cut the flash cards apart.

The following are just a few ideas of ways you may want to use these flashcards:

Ready-To-Use Ideas and Activities

Write some or all of the flashcard words on the chalkboard and divide the children into two or more groups. Now, as the children look over the list of words on the chalkboard, begin to describe any word from the list. Your description can be spelling characteristics, a definition, how the word makes you feel, whether it is a happy,sad, funny, or exciting word, or anything you can think of about the word. The team who guesses the word correctly first wins one point. After each word is guessed correctly cross it off of the list and go on to another word. You can either have the group try and guess the correct word working together or you can have one person at a time from each group be the guesser.

Use some or all of the flash cards and write one sentence for each card containing a blank where the flashcard word belongs. For example if the flashcard word is "birthday", the sentence could be, Marsha just turned 8 and last week she had a _____ party. Now, Divide the class into groups and hand out an equal number of sentences to each group. Also, give each group the flashcards that go with their sentences. Have each group complete the sentences by filling in the blank with the correct flashcard word. Tell the students not to write on the sentences you have handed out. They should rewrite the sentences on another sheet of paper. After each group is finished you can check the sentences to make sure they are correct then have groups exchange the sentences with the blanks in them and the flashcards that go with them.

Reproduce the bingo sheet on the opposite page in this book, making enough to have one for each student. Hand them out to the students. Take the flashcards and write the words on the chalk board. Have the students choose 24 of the words and write them in any order on the empty spaces of their bingo cards, writing only one word in each space. When all students have finished their cards, take the flashcards and make them in to a deck. Call out the words one at a time. Any student who has a word that you call out should make an "X" through the word to cross it out. The student who crosses out five words in a row first (Horizontally, vertically, or diagonally) wins the game. To extend the game you can continue playing until you a student crosses out all of the words on his bingo sheet.

Christopher Columbus

Christopher Columbus was born in Italy in 1451. He did not have much education. He was an adult before he learned to read and write. Columbus planned to sail around the world to India, a country in eastern Asia. Queen Isabella of Spain gave him the ships Pinta, Nina, and Santa Maria. In 1492 Columbus and his men set sail. It took them about two months before they saw land again. Columbus was sure he had sailed around the world to India. He had really sailed across the Atlantic Ocean and landed on some islands near North America! Columbus found people on the islands and called them Indians. He made three more trips from Spain to these new islands. He mapped the way so that other people could follow the same route. Columbus died in 1506, still believing he had reached Asia.

1. **What is the main idea of this story?**
    a. It took two months to reach land.
    b. Columbus named the Indians.
    c. Columbus found a way to America.
2. **Where was Columbus born?**

_____

3. **Who gave the ships to Columbus?**

_____

4. **What were the names of the ships?**

_____

5. **Why did Columbus name the new people "Indians"?**

_____

6. **How did Columbus help to develop North America?**

_____

_____

Think ahead: Look up Columbus in the encyclopedia. Find two new facts about him.

Reading Grade 3

Table Of Contents

Kelley Wingate products are available at fine educational supply stores throughout the U. S. and Canada.

Reading Comprehension   CD-3710   Printed in the United States Of America   ISBN 0-88724-428-9

Vocabulary Bingo

		FREE		

CD-3710

Name _____

Pocahontas

Pocahontas was an Indian Princess. Her father was the chief of a tribe. The tribe lived near Jamestown, an early English settlement in Virginia. Pocahontas was beautiful and very smart. In 1608 John Smith, a settler from Jamestown, was captured by the tribe. The Indians were going to kill him. Pocahontas saved his life. In 1613 Pocahontas was captured by the English. They taught her how they lived. She married a local farmer named John Rolfe. This helped the Indians and the English become friends. Pocahontas and John had a son. She took the baby to England to visit. Pocahontas became very popular in England. She became ill and died   there in 1617.

1. **What is the main idea of this story?**
   a. Pocahontas was an Indian.
   b. Pocahontas helped Indians and English become friends.
   c. Pocahontas died in England.
2. **What made Pocahontas a princess?**

_____

3. **How did she help John Smith?**

_____

4. **What happened when the English captured her?**

_____

5. **How did her marriage help the Indians and the English?**

_____

6. **How did Pocahontas help develop her country?**

_____

Think ahead: Look up Pocahontas in the encyclopedia. Find two new facts about her.

 CD-3710

John Cabot

John Cabot was born in Italy in 1451. He was a navigator, or sailor, and explorer. In 1497 King Henry VII of England hired John Cabot to find a way to the Orient (Japan and China). John crossed the Atlantic Ocean and landed in Canada. He called the area "New Found Land". The island he landed on is still called Newfoundland and is off the eastern coast of Canada. John Cabot explored this new land, looking for riches to take back to England. He sailed the coast as far south as Maine and north to Labrador, claiming the land for England. King Henry was pleased and sent Cabot on a second trip. Cabot was lost at sea in 1498 and was never seen again. The story of his first trip excited England and many other explorers came to Canada because of it.

1. **What is the main idea of this story?**
   a. John Cabot discovered Newfoundland.
   b. John Cabot was born in Italy.
   c. King Henry VII was pleased with John Cabot.

2. **In what year did Cabot land in Newfoundland?**

   _____

3. **Who hired Cabot to sail to the Orient?**

   _____

4. **Where is Newfoundland?**

   _____

5. **What happened on Cabot's second trip?**

   _____

6. **How did Cabot help develop the New World?**

   _____

   _____

   _____

Think ahead: Why is it hard to be the first person to explore a land no one knows about?

Benito Juarez

Benito Juarez was a Zapotec Indian born in 1806. His parents died when he was only three. He lived in a small village and did not go to school when he was young. When Benito was 12 he moved to the city of Oaxaca to live with his sister. He went to school and learned to speak Spanish. He grew up, studied law, and became a judge. In 1852 he became the governor, or leader, of Oaxaca. The Spanish and the French controlled much of Mexico at that time. Juarez began to fight for the rights of the Mexican people. He was exiled, or thrown out of the country, by President Santa Anna in 1853. He lived in New Orleans for two years and then returned to Mexico. Juarez was made President of Mexico in 1858. France invaded, or tried to take over, Mexico in 1862. Juarez lead his people in a fight against France and won. He remained President until he died in 1872.

1. **What is the main idea of this story?**
    a. Benito Juarez was an important Mexican leader.
    b. Benito Juarez was a Zapotec Indian.
    c. Juarez did not go to school until he was 12.
2. **What did Juarez study in school?**

_____

3. **When was Juarez the governor of Oaxaca?**

_____

4. **Where did Juarez live when he was exiled?**

_____

5. **When was Juarez made President of Mexico?**

_____

6. **What did Juarez fight for?**

_____

Think ahead: How was Benito Juarez important to the history of Mexico?

Jacques Cartier

After John Cabot lead the way to North America many explorers followed him. Jacques Cartier, a French sailor, came to Canada in 1534. Cartier discovered the St. Lawrence River. He found land covered with huge forests and lakes. The forests were full of animals that could be used for fur. Cartier returned to France and told about the many beaver he had found. Beaver fur was popular in France so traders were interested in Canada. Cartier returned to the New World and became friends with the Indians. He understood the Indians so he did not try to take the land away. Instead of trapping the beavers, Cartier traded metal tools and cloth for the skins. The Indians were happy with Cartier and stayed friendly with the French for over 100 years.

1. What is the main idea of this story?
  a. Cartier was from France.
  b. Cartier found fur for France.
  c. Cartier became friends with the Indians.

2. In what year did Cartier first come to Canada?

_____

3. What did Cartier find in the New World?

_____

4. Why did the Indians like Cartier?

_____

5. Why were French traders interested in Canada?

_____

6. What river did Cartier explore?

_____

Think ahead: What do you think might have happened if Cartier had taken the beaver rather than trading with the Indians?

Samuel de Champlain

France became interested in settling, or living in, the New World. In the early 1600's Samuel de Champlain came to North America to look for places where people could settle. Champlain explored the east coast of Canada and made the first map of the area. He explored and set up settlements in Nova Scotia and Maine. Champlain became friends with Huron Indians, helping them fight other Indian tribes. The Hurons helped him with fur trading and exploring. Champlain traveled down the St. Lawrence River and explored a beautiful lake which is now called Lake Champlain. The most important settlement Champlain began was called Quebec. Quebec became the capital of "New France", and is now the capital of the province of Quebec.

1. **What is the main idea of this story?**
    a. The Hurons liked Champlain.
    b. Champlain helped settle the eastern coast of Canada.
    c. A lake is named after Champlain.
2. **Why did Champlain come to the New World?**

_____

3. **What area did Champlain explore?**

_____

4. **How did Champlain help the Hurons?**

_____

_____

5. **What is the name of the area Champlain helped settle?**

_____

6. **What was the most important settlement founded by Champlain?**

_____

Think ahead: Find Lake Champlain on the map. What lands is it between?

Lewis and Clark

In the early 1800's most of the land west of the Mississippi River had not been explored. People wanted to find an easy way to cross the land and get to the Pacific Ocean. Two army officers, Merriweather Lewis and William Clark, were chosen to find a way. They began their trip from St. Louis in 1804. They took boats up the Missouri River, but the trip was very long and hard. They kept records of everything they saw and did. They spent the winter in the Rocky Mountains with Indians. The next spring an Indian woman named Sacajawea helped them to cross the mountains and go on to the ocean. They returned to St. Louis in 1806. Lewis and Clark had not found an easy route, but they had mapped the land. Now everyone knew what was between the Mississippi River and the Pacific Ocean.

1. **What is the main idea of this story?**
    a. Lewis and Clark were army officers.
    b. Sacajawea helped Lewis and Clark.
    c. Lewis and Clark explored and mapped the west.
2. **What did Lewis and Clark hope to find?**

_____

3. **Who helped them get through the Rocky Mountains?**

_____

4. **Where did their trip begin and end?**

_____

5. **How long did it take the men to get to the ocean and back?**

_____

6. **How did Lewis and Clark help to develop North America?**

_____

_____

_____

Think ahead: Look up Lewis and Clark in the encyclopedia. Find two new facts about them.

Sitting Bull

The Sioux Indians were a tribe that lived in the Great Plains area. Sitting Bull was their leader for many years. He was loved by his people because he was brave, kind, and wise. He protected his tribe from other Indians and settlers. He wanted others to know that Indians were part of the country and had a right to their own land. In the 1870's gold was discovered on Sioux land. People wanted the gold so the Army tried to take the land away. Sitting Bull helped defeat, or beat, the Army in a famous battle at Little Bighorn. Then he led his people to Canada to keep them safe. Sitting Bull came back to the United States and was put in prison for two years. Then he was allowed to return to the Sioux reservation, a place set aside just for the Indians. He died in 1890 when some Indians killed him.

1. **What is the main idea of this story?**
     a. Sitting Bull was a great Sioux leader.
     b. He led his people to a safe place in Canada.
     c. Sitting Bull helped at Little Bighorn.
2. **What tribe was Sitting Bull from?**

_____

3. **Why was he so loved by his tribe?**

_____

4. **Why did the army want to take away the Sioux land?**

_____

5. **Where did he take his tribe to save them?**

_____

6. **How did Sitting Bull die?**

_____

_____

Think ahead: Look up Sitting Bull in the encyclopedia. Find two new facts about him.

CD-3710

The Acadians

Many years ago the French had settled Acadia in Canada and the English had settled in the United States. England became interested in the northern land and wanted to settle there, too. In 1710 the two countries fought over Acadia and the English finally won. Acadia was renamed Nova Scotia. England said the French settlers could stay, but they had to be loyal, or faithful, to England. The Acadians did not want to do that so the English made them leave in 1755. The French Acadians were put on ships and sent to settle south, in the United States. The ships were very small, so the Acadians could not take much with them. They were scattered, or spread out, in the United States. Many families were parted and never saw each other again. Some of the Acadians found their way to a French settlement in Louisiana. They
settled there and became known as the Cajun people. Many Cajuns still live in southern Louisiana.

1. **What is the main idea of this story?**
     a. The English and French fought over Acadia.
     b. England won Acadia.
     c. French Acadians were moved to the United States.

2. **In what year did England win Acadia?**

_____

3. **Why were the French Acadians moved?**

_____

4. **Where were the Acadians sent?**

_____

5. **Why did the Acadians move to Louisiana?**

_____

_____

6. **What are the Acadians called today?**

_____

Think ahead: Why do you think the French Acadians moved instead of becoming part of England?

Harriet Tubman

Harriet Tubman was a slave. As a young girl she dreamed of freedom for her people. In 1849 Harriet escaped. She followed the North Star until she was safe in New York. For the next ten years Harriet made many trips back south. She helped hundreds of slaves escape, including her own parents. They used the Underground Railroad, a secret group of people who helped slaves pass safely to the north. When the Civil War began, Harriet helped the northern Army. She cooked, helped nurse the wounded, and even spied for the Army. When she died in 1913, Harriet was buried with full army honors.

1. **What is the main idea of this story?**
   - a. Harriet was a spy.
   - b. Harriet helped many slaves find freedom.
   - c. Harriet was a slave.
2. **How did Harriet escape?**

_____

3. **What was the Underground Railroad?**
   - a. A railroad that carried slaves.
   - b. A group that helped slaves escape to the north.
   - c. A tunnel to the north.
4. **How did Harriet help during the Civil War?**

_____

_____

5. **How was Harriet honored when she died?**

_____

6. **How did Harriet Tubman help people?**

_____

_____

_____

Think ahead: Look up Harriet Tubman in the encyclopedia. Find two new facts about her.

Clara Barton

Clara Barton was born in 1812. She was a school teacher for many years. She was over forty years old when the Civil War began. Clara helped care for the wounded soldiers. She helped set up hospitals near the battlefields. Clara worked hard to see that they had bandages, drugs, and other needed supplies. Soon she was known as "The Angel of the Battlefield". When she was fifty, Clara went to Europe to help in another war. While there she learned about the Red Cross, a group that helps take care of people during a war. Clara returned to the United States and started the American Red Cross. She became the first American Red Cross president in 1881, when she was almost sixty years old.

1. **What is the main idea of this story?**
    a. Clara Barton was a school teacher.
    b. Clara Barton was "The Angel of the Battlefield".
    c. Clara Barton helped during wars.
2. **What was Clara's first job?**

_____

3. **How did Clara help the wounded during the Civil War?**

_____

_____

4. **What was Clara's nickname?**

_____

5. **Where did she learn about the Red Cross?**

_____

6. **How did Clara Barton help people?**

_____

_____

_____

Think ahead: Look up Clara Barton in the encyclopedia. Find two new facts about her.

The Wright Brothers

Orville and Wilbur Wright were famous American brothers. They owned a bicycle shop in Dayton, Ohio. Although they were interested in bicycles, they also loved the idea of flying. In 1896 they began to experiment, or try new ideas, with flight. They started by testing kites and then gliders, which are motorless planes. These tests taught them how an airplane should rise, turn, and come back to earth. The brothers made over 700 glider flights at Kitty Hawk, a field in North Carolina. This was fun, but not good enough for them. Orville and Wilbur put a small engine on a plane they named Flyer I. On December 17, 1903 they took the first motor-powered flight that lasted about one minute. They continued to experiment until they could stay in the air for over one hour.

1. **What is the main idea of this story?**
   a. Testing new ideas is important.
   b. Flyer I was the first airplane.
   c. The Wright brothers were early pilots.
2. **What does the word "experiment" mean?**
   a. to try new ideas
   b. to test kites
   c. to stay in the air for one hour
3. **Where did the brothers test their gliders and plane?**

_____

4. **How long did the first motor-powered flight last?**

_____

5. **How did the brothers learn about what makes planes work?**

_____

6. **How did the Wright brothers help people?**

_____

_____

_____

Think ahead: Look up the Wright brothers in the encyclopedia. Find two new facts about them.

Amelia Earhart

Amelia Earhart was a famous woman pilot. She loved to fly planes. She was an early pioneer in American flight. In 1932 Amelia was the first person to fly alone from Newfoundland to Ireland. In 1935 she flew across the Pacific Ocean from Hawaii to California. In 1937 Amelia and her co-pilot, F.J. Noonan, tried to fly the equator all the way around the world. Their plane was lost and never found again. No one knows what happened to them. Some people think the plane crashed into the ocean. Others believe Amelia and Noonan were captured by the Japanese and that she is still alive today. Her last flight has been a famous mystery for over fifty years.

1. **What is the main idea of this story?**
    a. Amelia Earhart was a famous pilot.
    b. Amelia Earhart disappeared.
    c. Amelia Earhart was lost at sea.
2. **Who was Amelia Earhart?**

_____

3. **Why was her 1932 flight so important?**

_____

_____

4. **When did she fly from Hawaii to California?**

_____

5. **What two things do people believe might have happened to Amelia and Noonan?**

_____

_____

_____

_____

Think ahead: Look up Amelia Earhart in the encyclopedia. Find two new facts about her.

Thomas Edison

Thomas Alva Edison spent the first part of his life in Port Huron, Michigan. When he was in sixth grade his teacher said he was addled, not very smart, and so he quit school. Tom began to work selling newspapers and candy on a local railroad. He liked to experiment and spent all of his money on books and chemicals for his laboratory. When he was about eighteen he invented the automatic telegraph, a machine that sends messages. He began to invent other things and opened a business in New Jersey. Soon he had many people working on his ideas. In 1879 Edison invented the first lightbulb, a safer way to light homes and businesses. He later invented the phonograph, batteries, and the movie projector. By the time he died in 1931, Thomas Edison had over 1,000 inventions!

1. **What is the main idea of this story?**
   a. Thomas Edison quit school in the sixth grade.
   b. Edison invented the lightbulb.
   c. Thomas Edison was a great inventor.
2. **What does the word "addled" mean?**
   a. very smart
   b. not very smart
   c. a machine to send messages
3. **What was Edison's first invention?**

_____

4. **Name three other Edison inventions.**

_____

_____

5. **How did Thomas Edison help people?**

_____

_____

_____

Think ahead: Look up Thomas Edison in the encyclopedia. Find two new facts about him.

Henry Ford

Henry Ford was born in 1863 near Dearborn, Michigan. As a young boy he liked machines, and in 1890 he began to experiment with horseless carriages—the first cars. He built his first car in 1896. Each car had to be made by hand, so cars were difficult to build and cost a lot of money. Henry Ford figured out a way to make many cars at once. His invention became known as the assembly line. All the car parts were made and brought to a large, rolling belt. The parts were added on one piece at a time as the car rolled by on the belt. This process made cars easier to build and cost less money. Later on Henry designed the Model T Ford, which was a very popular car for many years.

1. **What is the main idea of this story?**
    a. Henry Ford made it easier to build cars.
    b. Henry Ford invented the first car.
    c. Henry Ford made the Model T.
2. **Where was Ford born?**

_____

3. **What made him famous?**

_____

4. **What was the horseless carriage?**
    a. an assembly line
    b. a car
    c. a rolling belt
5. **How did the assembly line work?**

_____

_____

6. **How did Henry Ford help people?**

_____

_____

Think ahead: Look up Henry Ford in the encyclopedia. Find two new facts about him.

Earth and Sun

The earth is a large round planet that circles around the sun. The top of the earth is the North Pole and the bottom is the south pole. A pretend line called an axis is the line that goes from the north pole through the earth to the South Pole. The earth spins on this axis. Put a stick through the middle of an apple and turn it. That is just like the earth's axis. The axis does not go straight up and down. It is tilted, or turned a little to one side. As the earth goes around the sun, sometimes the North Pole is closer to the sun than the South Pole. At that time it is summer in the north and winter in the south. When the earth gets to the other side of the sun, the South Pole is closer and has summer while the north pole has winter. This is how the earth gets seasons.

1. **What is the main idea of this story?**
    a. How the earth's tilt and the sun gives us seasons.
    b. The earth spins on an axis.
    c. Winter comes once a year.

2. **What is an axis?**

_____

_____

3. **When a pole is closest to the sun, what season is it?**

_____

4. **When a pole is farthest from the sun, what season is it?**

_____

5. **What is a word that means "turned to one side"?**
    a. axis
    b. tilted
    c. pole

6. **Why is it summer when we are nearer the sun?**

_____

_____

Think ahead: What happens when both poles are the same distance from the sun?

Summer

When the earth is tilted toward the sun we have a warm season or time of year that we call summer. During the summer it feels warmer because we are closer to the sun. Warm weather is a good time for plants to grow. They use the sun to make food and grow bigger. During the summer people wear lighter clothes to stay cool. They wear hats and sunglasses to protect themselves from the hot sun because it is easier to get sunburned during this hot season. We have more hours of sunlight and less hours of darkness during the summer. The longer days let us stay up later and enjoy the outdoors more.

1. **What is the main idea of this story?**
   a. Summers are hot.
   b. Wear hats to protect yourself from the sun.
   c. Summer is a season when we are closer to the sun.
2. **What does the word "season" mean?**
   a. warmer weather
   b. a time of year
   c. closer to the sun
3. **Why is the summer warmer than other seasons?**

_____

4. **Why do plants grow well during the summer?**

_____

5. **Why should people protect themselves from the sun?**

_____

6. **Are summer days longer or shorter? Why?**

_____

_____

_____

_____

Think ahead: Tell what you like to do during the summer season.

Plants

Plants eat and grow. They are living things. A plant has three main parts: roots, a stem, and leaves. Each part does an important job to keep the plant alive. The roots are the part of a plant that stays in the ground. Roots take in water and nutrients from the soil. The water and nutrients are what a plant uses for food. Roots also hold the plant up, keeping it from falling over. The stem of a plant is the main trunk. This part has the veins, or tubes, that carry food from the roots to the leaves. The leaves gather energy from the sun to help turn the nutrients into food. Leaves also take in carbon dioxide, a gas that plants breathe. Every plant also makes seeds so new plants can grow. Seeds of plants can be the nut, flower, vegetable, or fruit that grows on the plant.

1. **What is the main idea of this story?**
   a. Plants have veins.
   b. Plants get water through their roots.
   c. Plants have three main parts.
2. **What are the three main parts of a plant?**

_____

3. **What does each part do that helps keep the plant alive?**
a. _____

b. _____

c. _____
4. **What is another name for nutrients?**

_____

5. **What is carbon dioxide?**

_____

_____

_____

_____

Think ahead: Draw a picture of your favorite plant. Label the roots, stem, and leaves.

Fall

After summer comes the fall season. During this time of year our part of the world gets ready for winter. The weather becomes cooler. Leaves fall from the trees. The fruit, vegetables, and nuts of trees and plants are ripe and ready to pick. Animals gather seeds and nuts to store for the winter. Their fur grows longer and thicker to protect them from the cold. Some birds fly south to find warmer weather. People also gather food and store much of it for the winter. They get out sweaters and jackets to keep themselves warm as the weather becomes cooler. The hours of day and night are about equal during this season because we are moving away from the sun.

1. **What is the main idea of this story?**
   a. Animals prepare for colder weather.
   b. Fall is a cool season.
   c. People gather food for the winter.

2. **What happens to the weather in the fall?**

_____

_____

3. **What do animals do in the fall?**

_____

4. **How do people prepare for the fall?**

_____

5. **What happens to the days and nights?**

_____

6. **Why isn't the fall weather very hot or very cold?**

_____

_____

_____

Think ahead: Tell about some changes in plants you might have noticed in the fall.

Acorns

Oak trees grow nuts called acorns. These nuts are really the seeds of the oak tree. In the fall the acorns are ripe. Squirrels love to eat the acorns. They carry the nuts to their nests to eat. Squirrels also bury some acorns to save them for the winter. Sometimes the squirrels cannot remember where they buried the acorns. The nut stays in the ground all winter. In the spring the warm rain softens the shell and the acorn begins to grow. If nothing disturbs the new plant it will grow into a new oak tree.

1. What is the main idea of this story?
    a. Acorns are the seeds of oak trees.
    b. Squirrels love acorns.
    c. Spring rains make acorns grow.

2. An acorn is:
    a. the branch of an oak tree
    b. the seed of an oak tree
    c. a squirrels nest

3. How do acorns get into the ground?

_____

4. What are two uses for acorns?

_____

_____

5. Why do squirrels bury acorns?

_____

6. What happens if the buried acorn is not disturbed?

_____

_____

_____

_____

Think ahead: Draw a picture of an acorn on an oak tree.

Deciduous Trees

When fall comes the leaves of some trees change color and then fall to the ground. Trees that lose their leaves are called deciduous. Why do the leaves fall? A tree has veins, or tubes, like humans do. A tree's veins are filled with sap instead of blood. The sap carries water and minerals from the roots to the leaves. If the sap stayed in the branches all winter, it could freeze and the tree would die. Instead, the sap goes down into the roots where it will be warmer during the winter. Without sap the leaves cannot live, so they dry up and fall off. In the spring the sap goes back up to the branches and the tree grows new leaves.

1. **What is the main idea of this story?**
    a. Sap goes to the roots.
    b. Trees that lose their leaves are deciduous.
    c. Leaves dry up and fall off the trees.
2. **Deciduous means:**
    a. trees that lose their leaves
    b. branches without sap
    c. veins
3. **What does a tree have that is like our blood?**

_____

4. **Where does sap go for the winter? Why?**

_____

5. **Another word for vein is:**
    a. sap
    b. deciduous
    c. tube
6. **When does a deciduous tree grow new leaves?**

_____

_____

_____

_____

Think ahead: Draw a picture of a summer leaf and a fall leaf.

Winter

Winter is the season when your part of the earth is tilted away from the sun. The sun cannot warm the earth as well because it is further away. The air is much colder during this season. Many plants and animals protect themselves from the cold. Some plants push their sap into their roots and stop growing. Some animals hibernate, or go to sleep, in warm holes all winter. People heat their houses to stay warm. When they go outside they wear coats, mittens, and hats to protect them from the cold. Water from the clouds freezes and falls as snow. It covers the ground in a cold white blanket for the winter.

1. **What is the main idea of this story?**
   a. Winter is a cold season.
   b. Some animals hibernate.
   c. Snow covers the ground in winter.

2. **Why does the air get colder in winter?**

_____

_____

3. **How do plants protect themselves in winter?**

_____

_____

4. **A word that means "to sleep all winter" is:**
a. tilted
b. hibernate
c. protect

5. **How do people protect themselves in winter?**

_____

6. **Why does it snow in winter?**

_____

_____

Think ahead: Draw a picture of what you like to do during the winter season.

Snow

Snow is a form of water that falls from clouds during very cold weather. The cloud temperature must be freezing to make snow. Water vapor is frozen into tiny ice crystals in the cold air. The crystals join together to form a snowflake. Each snowflake has its own shape. No two are alike! The cold air keeps the snowflake from melting as it falls. The first snow of the season quickly melts, turns back into water, when it lands on the ground. That is because the ground is still warm from the summer and fall seasons. As more snow falls, it cools the earth and even freezes the top few inches. Now the snow will stay and build up until the sun is warm enough to melt it.

1. **What is the main idea of this story?**
   a. Snow is a crystal.
   b. Snow is very cold.
   c. How snow is made.
2. **What is snow?**

_____

3. **How does water change into snow?**

_____

4. **A word that means "to change water into ice" is:**
   a. melt
   b. freeze
   c. snow
5. **What does the word "melt" mean?**

_____

6. **Why does the first snow melt on the ground?**

_____

_____

_____

_____

Make a snowflake: Fold a piece of paper into a small square and cut shapes from the sides. Open it up to see your snowflake.

Spring

Spring is the season that comes after winter and before summer. Your part of the earth is turning back toward the sun. The snow melts and the air begins to warm again. Sap slowly climbs back into the trunk and branches of trees. New leaves begin to grow on plants. The ground thaws as it is warmed by the sun and melting snow. Animals come out of hibernation and look for food to eat. Spring brings a lot of rain that helps warm the earth. People take out umbrellas and put away their heavy winter clothes. The earth seems to wake up and begin to grow once again.

1. **What is the main idea of this story?**
   a. Spring warms the earth so things can grow.
   b. Snow melts in the spring.
   c. New leaves grow on plants.

2. **What is spring?**

_____

_____

3. **How do the plants wake up?**

_____

4. **A word that means "thaw" is:**
   a. rain
   b. unfreeze
   c. snow

5. **Why does your part of the earth begin to warm in the spring?**

_____

_____

6. **Why do people need umbrellas in the spring?**

_____

_____

Think ahead: Tell how the sun affects the earth for each of the four seasons.

27   CD-3710

Water Cycle

After a rainstorm you see a lot of puddles. The sun shines and the wind blows. Soon the puddles are gone. The sun and wind have turned the water into a gas called water vapor. This change from liquid to gas is called evaporation. As the water vapor rises with the air it sticks to small pieces of dust. As the air gets cooler the vapor changes back to water. This is called condensation. The dust and condensation gather together to form clouds. When there is too much water for the cloud to hold, the water falls back to the earth as precipitation, like rain or snow. This process of evaporation, condensation, and precipitation is called a water cycle.

1. **What is the main idea of this story?**
    a. How a water cycle works.
    b. Water can evaporate.
    c. Rain and snow are precipitation.

2. **How does water vapor get into the air?**

_____

_____

3. **What is condensation?**

_____

_____

4. **How does water vapor turn back into water?**

_____

_____

5. **What is a cloud?**

_____

_____

6. **What word means both rain and snow?**

_____

_____

_____

Think ahead: Draw a picture that shows how a water cycle works.

Clouds

Evaporated water, also called water vapor, rises in the air. Air high above the ground is cooler than air near the ground. When the water vapor meets the cooler air it condenses, changes back to water, on small pieces of dust. Each tiny piece of dust with water is called a droplet. A cloud is made of billions of droplets. There are many kinds of clouds. Some clouds form near the ground. These clouds are called fog and they make it hard to see very far. Some clouds are large and fluffy. They look like cotton balls in the sky. When a cloud gathers more water droplets than it can hold it becomes dark and is called a storm cloud. Some clouds are very high in the sky and look like feathers. These clouds are made of frozen water vapor, or tiny pieces of ice. Each type of cloud looks different, but they are all made from water vapor and dust.

1. **What is the main idea of this story?**
   a. A cloud is made of water droplets.
   b. Fog is a kind of cloud.
   c. There are many kinds of clouds.

2. **What is a cloud?**

_____

_____

3. **What is a storm cloud?**

_____

_____

4. **What do you call a cloud that is near the ground?**

_____

5. **What are high feathery clouds made of?**

_____

6. **How do clouds help the earth?**

_____

Think ahead: Draw a picture of the clouds you can see today.

Precipitation

Water that falls to the earth is called precipitation. Not all precipitation is rain. If the raindrops fall through air that is freezing, they will freeze and become sleet. When the temperature of the cloud is freezing the water droplets may form into tiny ice crystals. The crystals join together to make snowflakes. If the snowflakes fall through air that is also freezing, we will get snow. If the cloud droplets freeze into large balls of ice we may get hail. Rain, sleet, snow, and hail are all forms of precipitation.

1. **What is the main idea of this story?**
   a. There are ice crystals in clouds.
   b. There are different kinds of precipitation.
   c. Hail and snow are precipitation.

2. **Name four types of precipitation.**

   _____   _____

   _____   _____

3. **What is the cloud temperature when it snows?**

   _____

4. **What is the air temperature when it sleets or snows?**

   _____

5. **What is the temperature of the air and cloud when it rains?**

   _____

6. **What is hail?**

   _____

   _____

   _____

   _____

Think ahead: Draw the four types of precipitation.

Living Things

Some things are alive and some are not. A tree is alive. A rock is not alive. A robot can move and even talk, but it is not alive. How are living things different from things that are not alive? Here is how:

1. Living things can grow and change. An acorn grows into an oak tree. A baby grows into an adult.

2. All living things need energy. Energy is the ability to do work. Living things get energy from their food.

3. All living things can reproduce, or make new living things. A plant drops seeds so new plants will grow. Animals have babies or lay eggs.

1. What is the main idea of this story?
    a. Living things grow, need energy, and reproduce.
    b. Robots are not living things.
    c. Some things are alive and some are not.

2. What are three features that make living things different from things that are not alive?

_____   _____

_____

3. What word means "to make new living things"?
    a. energy
    b. reproduce
    c. alive

HI!

4. A robot uses energy. Why isn't it alive?

_____

_____

5. A cloud can grow and change. Why isn't it alive?

_____

_____

Think ahead: Make a list of six things that are alive and six things that are not alive.

Energy

Whenever something moves or changes, energy is being used. When wood burns or water turns to ice, it takes energy. Energy means being able to do work. There are different forms of energy. One form is heat energy. If you put a pot of water on a heated stove, when it is hot enough, the water will begin to boil. When you take the heat away, the water cools and stops boiling. Light is an important form of energy. Plants use light to grow. We use light to see. Without light we could not live.   Another form of energy is sound. Sounds are caused by things that vibrate, or move quickly back and forth. A drum vibrates when it is hit. The vibrations reach your ears and you hear the sound.   Much of the energy we use is stored in other things. The food we eat has stored energy that helps us to walk, talk, and live. Energy is what makes the world move!

1. **What is the main idea of this story?**
   a. Energy is used to change or move things.
   b. Light is energy.
   c. Energy can be stored.

2. **Where do plants get most of their energy?** _____

_____

3. **When a piano is played, what kind of energy does it make?**

_____

4. **What are the kinds of energy this story talks about?**

_____

_____

5. **What is energy used for?**

_____

_____

_____

Think ahead: Make a list of four things that use energy and four things that make energy.

The Sun

At night the sky is full of stars. Stars are burning balls of gases that give off heat and light energy. The stars look small and we cannot feel any of their heat because they are so far away. One star that we can see and feel the heat from is our sun. We are close enough to have the heat energy from the sun warm our earth. The sun's light makes our days bright and gives plants energy to grow. The sun is the most important star for the earth. If it were too far away the earth would grow cold and plants would die. If the sun were too close to the earth it would be so hot that things would burn and die. It is nice that our star is right where it is!

1. **What is the main idea of this story?**
    a. The sun is a star.
    b. Earth is too far from other stars.
    c. We can see and feel the sun.
2. **What is a star?**

_____

3. **Why can't we feel the heat from other stars?**

_____

4. **What kinds of energy do we get from the sun?**

_____

5. **What would happen if the sun were closer or further from the earth?**

_____

6. **Why is the sun so important to the earth?**

_____

_____

_____

_____

_____

Think ahead: What might happen to the earth if the sun ever burns out?

Climate

The climate of an area is the usual weather it has over a long time. North America has very different climates from area to area. The northern areas are closer to the North Pole than the equator. They have mild summers (not harsh or too warm) and long winters that are filled with ice and snow. The southern areas have long hot summers and mild winters because they are closer to the equator. The southwestern areas have a dry climate. They do not get a lot of rainfall. Both the eastern and western coasts have heavy rainfall. The climate of an area affects, or changes, how people live. It helps us decide what kind of houses to live in or what type of clothes to wear.

1. The main idea of this story is:
    a. Many areas have mild winters.
    b. Climate affects the way we live.
    c. Climate is the weather an area has during the year.

2. Why do the northern parts of North America have long winters?

_____

3. Why do the southern parts of North America have long summers?

_____

4. What does the word "mild" mean?
    a. gentle, not harsh
    b. hot
    c. dry

5. Which area has a dry climate?

_____

_____

6. How does the climate affect the way we live?

_____

_____

Think ahead: What kind of climate do you live in? How does it affect you?

Making a Living

The kind of climate we live in can affect how we make a living.   In some parts of the country the weather makes the soil, or dirt, good for certain growing crops. In other areas it is difficult to grow much of anything. The low, wet lands may be good for crops such as rice or sugar cane. Drier land is good for corn or wheat. Grasslands are best for raising cattle or sheep. People who live in dry desert areas will not be able to grow fields of crops. They will have to make their living some other way. Some mountain areas are good for crops like tobacco but not rice or wheat.   Other mountain areas are best for mining coal or other minerals. Where you live may affect the type of job you do.

1. **The main idea of this story is:**
    a. Some soil is good for growing crops.
    b. Climate may affect how we make a living.
    c. Mining is done in the mountain areas.
2. **What crops grow well in low, wet areas?**

_____

3. **What type of area would you live in to raise cows?**

_____

4. **What does the word "soil" mean?**
    a. climate
    b. metal
    c. dirt
5. **Where might you live if you were a miner?**

_____

6. **How does the climate affect the way we make a living?**

_____

_____

_____

_____

Think ahead: How does the climate affect jobs in the community where you live?

Farming

Farming is one important way of making a living. Farming gives people the food they need. The climate helps farmers know what crops to plant. Crops like wheat, corn, vegetables, and fruits are grown on farms. The food they grow will usually be canned or frozen so it can be shipped to other places. This way, people can buy the food they need in grocery stores. Climate also tells farmers when to plant the crop. If crops are planted too early, frost (tiny ice crystals) might ruin the plants. If there is too little or too much rainfall the crops may be ruined. If a crop is planted too late, there may not be enough time for it to grow before winter comes. Farmers know the climate and watch the weather to grow the best crops they can.

1. The main idea of this story is:
   a. Farmers grow food.
   b. Wheat and vegetables are crops.
   c. Climate has a big effect on farming.

2. Why is farming important to us?

_____

3. How do people in other places get some of the crops?

_____

4. What does the word "frost" mean?
a. ice crystals
b. snow
c. heavy rain

5. How does climate affect when a crop is planted?

_____

_____

6. Why do farmers think about the climate before they plant crops?

_____

_____

Think ahead: What crops are grown in your area?

36

Ranching

Ranching is another important way of making a living. A ranch is different from a farm. A farmer grows plants while a rancher raises, or grows, animals. Cattle, sheep, goats, and pigs are raised on ranches. These animals give us meat or other products we use every day. Some ranchers have milk cows. They are milked every day. The milk is made into cheese, cream, butter, and milk. Other ranchers raise cows for the meat and leather. These cows are butchered, or killed, to give us meat to eat. The hides, or skin, are used to make leather products like belts, purses, and shoes. Goat and sheep ranchers shear, or cut the hair and wool, from their animals. The hair is sold and made into yarn and cloth for us to wear. Some sheep and pigs, like some cows, are grown for their meat. All of these animals, and the ranches they live on, are important to our lives.

1. **The main idea of this story is:**
   a. Ranches grow animals.
   b. Ranches give us products we use every day.
   c. Sheep and cows are raised on ranches.
2. **Why is ranching important to us?**

_____

3. **What products do we get from cows?**

_____

4. **What does the word "shear" mean?**
   a. kill
   b. skin
   c. cut
5. **What is another word for "skin of an animal"?**
   a. butcher
   b. hide
   c. to cut wool
6. **What products do we get from sheep?**

_____

_____

Think ahead: What products have you used today that came from a ranch?

Mining

In some parts of the world we can find minerals. Minerals are solid materials that are made by nature. Some minerals are oil, coal, and diamonds. Mining, or digging out, the minerals is one way to make a living. Oil is used in many ways. We use oil to make gasoline, ink, paints, plastics, and even lipstick! Oil is mined by deep wells that are dug into the earth. Other minerals, like coal and diamonds, are mined by digging large tunnels into the earth. Men go into the tunnels and remove the minerals so we can use them for many different things. Some minerals are ores, or metals, and are also mined. Iron, copper, silver, and gold are ores that are smelted, or melted, to make metal. If these minerals were not mined, we would not have many of the products we use every day!

1. **The main idea of this story is:**
   a. We mine minerals to make many products.
   b. Oil is a useful mineral.
   c. Minerals help us in many ways.

2. **Why is mining important to us?**

_____

3. **How is oil mined?**

_____

4. **What does the word "smelt" mean?**
   a. metal
   b. melt ores into metal
   c. to dig tunnels

5. **How are most minerals mined?**

_____

6. **Name some products that are made from oil.**

_____

_____

_____

Think ahead: What products do you use that are made from minerals?

Lumbering

Many things are made of wood. Tables, doors, homes, and paper are all made of wood. The job of getting the wood to make products is called lumbering. Lumbering in North America was first started in the northern forests. New England, New York, and Michigan had huge forests that were cleared, or cut, to make lumber. As these forests were used up, lumbering was done in the Appalachian Mountains and in the southeastern area. Today a lot of our lumber comes from the forests in the northwestern states. People who make a living cutting trees are called lumberjacks. The logs they cut are floated down rivers or trucked to sawmills where they are cut into boards, planks, and beams.

1. The main idea of this story is:
    a. Lumberjacks cut trees.
    b. Many products are made of wood.
    c. Lumbering is how we get wood for products.

2. Why is lumbering important to us?

_____

3. Where did most of the early lumbering take place?

_____

4. What does the word "cleared" mean?
    a. cut away
    b. lumber
    c. wood

5. How might climate affect where people get lumber?

_____

_____

6. How do cut trees get to sawmills?

_____

_____

_____

Think ahead: Name six things in your classroom that are made from wood.

Manufacturing

Most people in North America make a living by manufacturing. To manufacture means to make a product. Nearly everything we use has been manufactured in a factory. Food products are canned, boxed, or frozen in factories before they are shipped to grocery stores. Clothing, cars, and chemicals are made in factories. Computers, pencils, and carpets are manufactured. Some factories are very small and can be run by one family. Many factories are very large and make thousands of products every day.

1. **The main idea of this story is:**
    a. Most products we use have been manufactured.
    b. Factories manufacture goods.
    c. Food products are made in factories.
2. **Why is manufacturing important to us?**

_____

_____

3. **Name five products that are manufactured?**

_____

_____

_____

4. **What word means "to make a product"?**
    a. manufacture
    b. factory
    c. products
5. **How do most of the people in your country make a living?**

_____

_____

_____

Think ahead: Name six things in your classroom that were manufactured.

Services

Many people make a living by selling their services to others. A service is work done for other people. Teachers, doctors, librarians, and bus drivers are service people. Waitresses, babysitters, and cab drivers are also service people. Many service people work for the government.   Mail carriers, police officers, and firefighters work for the government. The leader of a government has a service job, too! It would be difficult to get through a day without the services these people provide, or give us.

1. The main idea of this story is:
    a. A doctor has a government job.
    b. Services help us every day.
    c. Teachers have service jobs.
2. Why are services important to us?

_____

3. What does the word "service" mean?
    a. work for pay
    b. help others
    c. work done for others
4. Name four service jobs that are not listed in this passage.

_____

_____

5. What is a word that means "to supply or give"?
    a. service
    b. government
    c. provide
6. What are three government service jobs?

_____

_____

_____

Think ahead: Name three services your family has used this week?

Transportation

When North America was first developed, you could move across the continent by taking a wagon pulled by horses or oxen. It took months to travel from Toronto to California. You may have taken a ship, but it had to go around the whole continent and took even longer than the wagons. In 1869 railroads finally connected the east coast to the west coast. It became easier to travel and ship goods from one place to another. Today, highways and fast cars, trucks, or buses make it easy to go almost anywhere in just a few days. Airplanes can make the trip in just a few hours. All of these ways of getting from one place to another are forms of transportation. We use transportation to make life easier as we go to work, ship goods from one area to another, or visit with distant family.

1. **The main idea of this story is:**
   a. Transportation makes life easier.
   b. It took a long time to travel from one coast to another
   c. Cars, trains, and airplanes are forms of transportation.
2. **Why were railroads easier to travel by than wagons or ships?**

_____

3. **What two ways did early settlers get from one side of the United States to the other?**

_____

4. **What does the word "transportation" mean?**
   a. ways to travel
   b. trucks
   c. trains and airplanes
5. **How did the railroad make travel easier?**

_____

_____

6. **Why do we need fast ways to get to far places?**

_____

_____

Think ahead: What forms of transportation have you used this week?

Communication

How do we communicate, or share information, with each other? We can talk to our parents and tell them about our day. We can use the telephone to talk to people in other places. We can listen to the radio and hear about things that are happening anywhere in the country or world! Talking is only one way to communicate. Newspapers, books, and magazines are also types of communication. We can share information by reading about it in print. We can find out about the past, about how to make things, or about science by reading what other people wrote in books. The television is a kind of communication that is almost like being there. Reporters show us live pictures and tell us what is happening in our community, country, and world. We can see what is happening without having to be there. Communication is a way of sharing information so that we all can learn what is happening anywhere in the world.

1. **The main idea of this story is:**
    a. Television is the best form of communication
    b. Books and newspapers are kinds of communication
    c. Communication lets us share information
2. **Why is communication important to us?**

_____

3. **How can we learn what is happening in other parts of the world?**

_____

4. **What does the word "communicate" mean?**
    a. speak
    b. share information
    c. watch television
5. **Name five kinds of communication.**

_____

_____

6. **Why is it important to have communication with the rest of the world?**

_____

_____

Think ahead: How could you communicate with a child in another country

Foods

Years ago people ate only the foods that were found nearby. Transportation was not very good so food could not be shipped long distances. Because of this, food was not the same everywhere in the country. People in the north did not have fresh fruit or vegetables during the winter months. People in Illinois did not get oranges or grapefruit because they could not grow them. Today trains, trucks, and airplanes carry fresh food to many areas. You can eat a Washington apple in Mississippi. You can have Florida oranges in Ontario. You can eat Maine lobster in Montreal. It is even possible to find food and spices from other countries in your local, or nearby, grocery store! Now everyone can have the food they need or want at any time of the year.

1. **The main idea of this story is:**
   a. Better transportation helps us get fresh food.
   b. Food could not be shipped far or it would spoil.
   c. Food is important to us.
2. **How did people used to get food?**

_____

_____

3. **How do people get fresh food from other places?**

_____

_____

4. **What word means "nearby"?**
   a. possible
   b. transportation
   c. local
5. **Why do we need to have foods from other places?**

_____

_____

6. **Why might we want foods from other countries?**

_____

_____

Think ahead: What foods from other countries can you find in your grocery store?

     CD-3710

Homes

Are all homes the same? No, people live in many different kinds of homes. Some people have large homes with big yards. Others live in apartments with no yard at all. Houses do not all look the same. They are not all made from the same materials, or supplies, either.   Some houses are made of wood. Others are made of brick or stone. The climate of an area affects how homes are designed, or planned. Homes in the northern areas are built with insulated, or padded, walls to keep the cold out. Most homes in the southern areas have air conditioning, or cooling systems, to protect them from the hot summers. Homes that are near rivers or swamps that flood in the spring are often built on stilts off the ground. When the water rises, the homes are kept safe above it all. Homes that are built to fit the climate are much more comfortable to live in!

1. **The main idea of this story is:**
   a. Homes are built differently.
   b. All homes are the same.
   c. Some homes are made of wood and others of brick.
2. **Why are homes important to us?**

_____

3. **What does the word "design" mean in this passage?**
   a. color
   b. plan
   c. draw
4. **What is another word for "padded"?**
   a. insulated
   b. comfortable
   c. cooled
5. **Why do homes in the south need to be air conditioned?**

_____

6. **Why don't we build all homes alike?**

_____

_____

Think ahead: What special features does your home have that protects you from the climate?

Clothing

The clothes we wear are much the same all over the country. We all have shirts, pants, dresses, and socks. However, the climate we live in does cause us to wear certain things more often than we would if we lived somewhere else. It also helps us choose the materials we use to make the clothes. In cold climates people dress to keep warm. Wool from sheep is clipped and made into yarn for sweaters or cloth for warm clothes. In warm climates, people wear lighter clothing. Cotton is grown in warm parts of our country and we use it to make cool, comfortable shirts and slacks. Silk, another lightweight material, comes from the silkworm. We usually get silk from other countries like China or Japan. In wet climates most people have raincoats and boots handy to protect them from the rain. Many of the things we use to protect us from the rain are made from rubber or plastic. Rubber comes from trees in tropical, or very hot and wet, places. We use rubber for boots and shoe bottoms. Plastic is made in factories. Many umbrellas and raincoats are made from plastic. Plastic is also used to make nylon and rayon, materials that are used for many different kinds of clothes.

1. The main idea of this story is:
   a. Plastic is used in many materials.
   b. Wool is used in colder climates.
   c. Clothing helps protect us from the climate.

2. How does the climate affect what we wear?

_____

3. Where does silk come from?

_____

4. What does the word "tropical" mean?
   a. a kind of plastic
   b. rainy
   c. hot and wet

5. Where does rubber come from?

_____

6. Why do we use different materials to make our clothes?

_____

_____

_____

Think ahead: What kind of clothes do you need for the climate you live in?

Harming the Earth

We have learned that we use many things from the earth. Minerals, trees, water, and plants are resources (things that take care of our needs) that we get from the earth. We use the resources to make life better for ourselves. We must also be careful not to ruin the earth by abusing, or misusing, these resources. A farmer must rotate, or change, crops every few years or he can ruin the soil. Lumberjacks must plant new trees to replace the ones they cut or we will run out of trees before long. Manufacturers cannot dump chemicals into rivers or bury them because they may poison our water and soil. The earth gives us so much. We must be careful not to waste our resources. We must conserve (take care of and protect) our natural resources so that they will be here for years to come.

1. The main idea of this story is:
   a. We must protect the earth by conserving our resources.
   b. The earth gives us natural resources.
   c. Manufacturers are ruining our water and land.

2. How are natural resources important to us?

_____

3. What is another word for "misusing"?
   a. resources
   b. abusing
   c. conserving

4. What does the word "rotate" mean?
   a. change
   b. replant
   c. soil

5. Name two ways we can abuse our resources.

_____

_____

6. Name two ways we can conserve resources.

_____

_____

Think ahead: What are some ways your community tries to conserve resources?

Ecology

The study of living things and how they depend on the world around them is called ecology.   People depend on the earth to provide natural resources. We use the resources to live and to make our lives easier. Nature can keep itself balanced (even or steady) if left alone. People have to use the plants and animals for food and materials they need to survive. People also destroy many plants and animal carelessly. They cut down rain forests to use the trees, destroying plants and animals that help keep nature balanced. People throw trash in the oceans and poison our water and land with chemicals that are no longer useable. Nature is not able to get rid of the waste as fast as we dump it. We must be careful with the way we use the earth, or we may end up without the resources we need.

1. The main idea of this story is:
  a. Man depends on resources.
  b. The earth cannot get rid of our waste fast enough.
  c. Man must learn to use nature wisely.

2. What is ecology?

_____

_____

3. How are people ruining the earth?

_____

4. What does the word "balanced" mean?
  a. resources
  b. even or steady
  c. survive

5. Can we stop using resources?

_____

_____

6. What can we do to help nature stay balanced?

_____

_____

Think ahead: What may happen if man continues to waste natural resources?

Using Context Clues

When you come to a word you don't know, use the **context clues** (other words around it) to help you figure out the meaning.

Use context clues to figure out the meaning of each underlined word below.
Circle the correct meaning.

1. The green light coming from the haunted house was frightening. It was an <u>eerie</u> sight!
    a. green   b. spooky   c. funny

2. The man <u>bellows</u> at his family when he gets very angry.
    a. laughs   b. eats   c. shouts

3. The <u>clasp</u> of the seatbelt was not fastened correctly.
    a. buckle   b. strap   c. seat

4. We must leave soon. We will <u>depart</u> as soon as everyone is ready.
    a. watch   b. leave   c. sign

5. I have an <u>errand</u> to do for my mother. She wants me to go to the store for her.
    a. job   b. bag   c. test

6. When my sister found out I broke her toy, she was <u>furious</u> with me.
    a. very pleased   b. very tired   c. very angry

7. Your must <u>insert</u> a nickel in the machine to get a gum ball.
    a. put in   b. take out   c. hand over

8. Jack is asleep in class. <u>Nudge</u> him with your elbow to wake him up.
    a. sweep   b. signal   c. push

Using Context Clues

When you come to a word you don't know, use the **context clues** (other words around it) to help you figure out the meaning.

Use context clues to figure out the meaning of each underlined word below.
Circle the correct meaning.

1. We need another <u>plank</u> for the floor of our clubhouse. It should be about six feet long.
      a. nail   b. board   c. hammer

2. My new sweater is the most <u>recent</u> style. It was just designed last week.
      a. oldest   b. newest   c. youngest

3. I was so embarrassed, my face turned <u>crimson</u>.
      a. red   b. white   c. cold

4. I really <u>blundered</u> when I gave the wrong answer on the test.
      a. danced   b. laughed   c. made a mistake

5. The children <u>clustered</u> around their teacher when they went into the snake exhibit. Most of them were a little scared.
      a. jumped   b. slept   c. gathered

6. We are on the second floor. You must <u>descend</u> the stairs to get to the first floor.
      a. go down   b. go up   c. go around

7. The children were <u>exhausted</u> after running five miles.
      a. awake   b. tired   c. ready to run

8. Would you quickly <u>sketch</u> a house for me. Use white paper and a pencil.
      a. build   b. draw   c. play

Using Context Clues

When you come to a word you don't know, use the **context clues** (other words around it) to help you figure out the meaning.

Use context clues to figure out the meaning of each underlined word below. Circle the correct meaning.

1. **His mouth was <u>gaping</u> when he yawned.**
   a. wide open   b. closed   c. smiling

2. **Katie was a <u>loyal</u> friend. She would not tell my secret even when they called her names.**
   a. mean   b. playful   c. true

3. **My arm was <u>numb</u> after I slept on it all night.**
   a. unfeeling   b. thick   c. important

4. **We used an old rag to <u>plug</u> the hole in the boat. That kept the water from coming in.**
   a. to cut out   b. to stop up   c. to paint

5. **I will <u>release</u> your hand if you promise not to write on me.**
   a. let go of   b. twist   c. hold

6. **Don't <u>dawdle.</u> We must be ready in just five minutes!**
   a. waste time   b. hurry   c. get dressed

7. **Tie your new <u>bonnet</u> under your chin. It will shade your head from the hot sun.**
   a. umbrella   b. coat   c. hat

8. **We must <u>crate</u> the dishes so they won't break in the moving van.**
   a. box   b. make   c. drop

Using Context Clues

When you come to a word you don't know, use the **context clues** (other words around it) to help you figure out the meaning.

Use context clues to figure out the meaning of each underlined word below. Circle the correct meaning.

1. I <u>detest</u> having my teeth pulled!
    a. enjoy   b. hate   c. fix

2. Take the lid off the box and <u>expose</u> what is inside so we can all see.
    a. uncover   b. break   c. send

3. Jason fell off his bike when he rode in the loose <u>gravel</u>. The sharp edges cut his knees.
    a. sand   b. pebbles   c. grass

4. It had not rained in a long time. It was so dry that the <u>sod</u> in my front yard was turning brown.
    a. sand   b. pebbles   c. grass

5. <u>Observe</u> the bird and see if you can find where she hid her nest.
    a. study   b. call to   c. feather

6. My sister took her time easing into the cold water. I <u>plunged</u> right in.
    a. waded   b. sat   c. dived

7. This job <u>requires</u> a hammer and nails.
    a. needs   b. looks at   c. sits down

8. The <u>jagged</u> edge of the broken window was dangerous.
    a. pointed   b. smooth   c. easy

Using Context Clues

When you come to a word you don't know, use the **context clues** (other words around it) to help you figure out the meaning.

Use context clues to figure out the meaning of each underlined word below. Circle the correct meaning.

1. **Please keep your answer <u>brief</u>. A "yes" or "no" is enough.**
   a. long   b. fancy   c. short

2. **The boy was <u>cruel</u> to the dog. He beat it with a stick.**
   a. mean   b. nice   c. kind

3. **Frank wore fake glasses and a wig. He <u>disguised</u> himself.**
   a. painted   b. hid   c. liked

4. **Do not leave your swimsuit in the sun because the colors may <u>fade</u>.**
   a. lose color   b. darken   c. wave

5. **Bill was full of <u>grief</u> when his dog ran away. He cried himself to sleep.**
   a. happiness   b. anger   c. sadness

6. **Do not <u>mingle</u> your crayons with mine. I don't want to get any of yours by mistake.**
   a. bend   b. mix together   c. use

7. **A wonderful <u>odor</u> was coming from the kitchen while mother baked cookies.**
   a. taste   b. sound   c. smell

8. **Evie put her money in the <u>pouch</u> she wore on her belt.**
   a. bag   b. paper   c. shirt

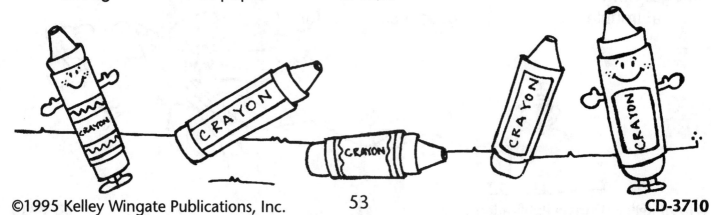

Using Context Clues

When you come to a word you don't know, use the **context clues** (other words around it) to help you figure out the meaning.

Use context clues to figure out the meaning of each underlined word below.
Circle the correct meaning.

1. Joe did not <u>respond</u> when Alice asked him a question. He was asleep and did not hear her.
      a. answer   b. read   c. eat

2. The icy sidewalk was so <u>slick</u>, Ann fell down when she stepped on it.
      a. wet   b. pretty   c. slippery

3. Use the big <u>shears</u> to cut that paper.
      a. ruler   b. scissors   c. pencil

4. The fox had a <u>cunning</u> plan to catch the rabbit.
      a. clever   b. cloudy   c. fast

5. Six brown puppies were on <u>display</u> in the pet store window.
      a. put out for show   b. digging   c. furry

6. Mother told me I did a great job. She knows how to <u>flatter</u> me.
      a. holler at   b. praise   c. smile

7. A <u>gust</u> of wind took my kite higher than ever before!
      a. small   b. storm   c. blast

8. The small boy got into a lot of <u>mischief</u> at school. His mother had to come and get him.
      a. trouble   b. goodness   c. fun

Using Context Clues

When you come to a word you don't know, use the **context clues** (other words around it) to help you figure out the meaning.

Use context clues to figure out the meaning of each underlined word below. Circle the correct meaning.

1. I try to <u>avoid</u> things I don't like.
    a. get close to   b. stay away from   c. eat

2. We must use <u>caution</u> when crossing a busy street.
    a. feet   b. hurry   c. be careful

3. The kitten had <u>dainty</u> little feet. They were tinier than my thumb!
    a. small   b. furry   c. nice

4. I <u>dodged</u> when my brother threw the towel at my face.
    a. ducked down   b. smiled   c. got wet

5. The mother was <u>frantic</u> when her little girl was lost in the store.
    a. wild with worry   b. a little upset   c. laughing

6. It is not a good day to be outside. The snow and wind are <u>harsh</u>.
    a. bright and pretty   b. windy and mild   c. cutting and sharp

7. It rained last night. I can tell because the ground is still <u>moist</u>.
    a. dry   b. wet   c. warm

8. Andy had to go pick up his <u>parcel</u> at the post office. It was too large to fit in his mailbox.
    a. package   b. stamps   c. bills

Using Context Clues

When you come to a word you don't know, use the **context clues** (other words around it) to help you figure out the meaning.

Use context clues to figure out the meaning of each underlined word below. Circle the correct meaning.

1. **The farmer wore <u>overalls</u> to protect his clothes from the dusty fields.**
   a. plastic boots   b. loose pants with a bib and straps   c. a large hat

2. **The kitten <u>pounced</u> on the rubber ball, trapping it between her paws.**
   a. hit   b. jumped   c. danced

3. **I don't like that <u>remark</u> you made about my new dress.**
   a. comment   b. look   c. drink

4. **I am <u>baffled</u> about who took my bicycle. There are no clues to help me figure it out!**
   a. angry   b. puzzled   c. happy

5. **Do not <u>char</u> my steak. I don't like meat that is too well done.**
   a. cook   b. eat   c. burn

6. **Buy the book now. It is the last one, and if you <u>delay</u> even one day it may be gone.**
   a. put off; wait   b. walk   c. ask

7. **I was so tired, I <u>dozed</u> off for a few minutes.**
   a. ran   b. fell asleep   c. read

8. **This blouse has too many <u>frills</u> on the sleeves. I like clothes to be plain.**
   a. ruffles   b. buttons   c. cotton

Using Context Clues

When you come to a word you don't know, use the **context clues** (other words around it) to help you figure out the meaning.

Use context clues to figure out the meaning of each underlined word below. Circle the correct meaning.

1. Ann wasn't sure which way to go. She <u>hesitated</u> for a moment, trying to decide.
     a. chose quickly   b. turned around   c. paused or stopped to think

2. Molly put her hand over her mouth to <u>muffle</u> the sneeze. She hoped no one heard it.
     a. silence   b. make louder   c. help

3. I will not <u>permit</u> students to cheat on a test!
     a. help   b. allow   c. push

4. The tree was quickly dragged off the road. Now we can <u>proceed</u>.
     a. cut up   b. sleep   c. go on

5. Cats <u>prey</u> upon mice and birds.
     a. play with   b. hunt and kill   c. like

6. Water is <u>scarce</u> in the desert.
     a. hard to find   b. easy to see   c. all around

7. Guards, <u>seize</u> the thief before he can escape!
     a. help   b. punish   c. grab

8. Apple pie is my favorite pie. I will <u>savor</u> every bite!
     a. hate   b. enjoy   c. give away

Using Context Clues

When you come to a word you don't know, use the **context clues** (other words around it) to help you figure out the meaning.

Use context clues to figure out the meaning of each underlined word below. Circle the correct meaning.

1. **The cookies are all gone. Can we make a new <u>batch</u> today?**
   a. recipe   b. group   c. roll

2. **I was so nervous, my hands got <u>clammy</u>.**
   a. long   b. hot   c. sweaty

3. **I <u>dread</u> going to bed each night. It is dark and scary in my room.**
   a. am afraid of   b. enjoy   c. want

4. **The puppies love to <u>frolic</u> in the grass.**
   a. sleep   b. dig   c. run and play

5. **The children were frightened by the storm, so they <u>huddled</u> under the covers of their bed.**
   a. slept   b. crowded together   c. played

6. **The clown <u>murmured</u> so low no one could hear what he said.**
   a. tumbled   b. hopped   c. whispered

7. **Ken was so upset his lower lip began to <u>quiver</u> and he looked like he was going to cry.**
   a. shake   b. bite   c. get wet

8. **The <u>scent</u> of the perfume was so strong we all began to cough.**
   a. bottle   b. price   c. smell

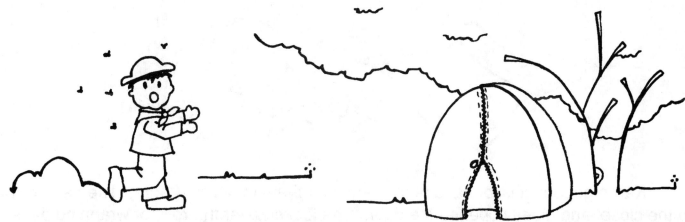

Joe stopped on the trail. He wiped the sweat from his face and sighed. It was a warm day and his backpack was beginning to feel heavy. A mosquito buzzed near Joe's neck. He swatted the bug before it could bite him. This trip was not as easy as he had thought it would be. The trail was clearly marked, so Joe knew he wouldn't get lost among the trees. There were so many hills that tired his legs. His long pants protected him from insects, but they also made his legs hot. Joe rested for a minute, taking a long drink from his water bottle. "I will get to the camp soon," thought Joe. "I have to prove to the other scouts that I am strong. I really want to earn my trail blazing badge."

1. Where is Joe?

_____

2. What clues tell you about where Joe is?

_____

3. Where is Joe going?

_____

4. How did Joe know he couldn't get lost?

_____

5. Why was Joe so hot?

_____

6. What would be a good title for this story?

_____

The Surprise

Karen got out scissors and tape. She took them to her bedroom. Then she went to the closet and quietly opened the door. She looked over the rolls of wrapping paper and chose the green one with yellow horns and party blowers printed on it. Karen quietly closed the door and tip-toed back to her room. She closed and locked the bedroom door. Safe at last! Karen pulled a paper bag from under her bed. She was careful not to rattle the paper too much. She didn't want her sister to hear what she was doing. Karen had saved her allowance for five weeks to buy the red sweater that was in the bag. It was such a beautiful sweater. Her sister had really liked it when they saw it for the first time in the store window. Karen carefully wrapped the sweater in the green paper. She signed the card and taped it to the package. What a good surprise this would be!

1. Where does most of this story take place?

_____

2. Why was Karen being so quiet?

_____

3. Who is the sweater for?

_____

4. What clues tell you who the sweater is for?

_____

5. How long had Karen saved to buy the sweater?

_____

6. What do you think is the reason Karen is trying to surprise her sister?

_____

The Contest

Marcie's face was red and tears stung her eyes. She blinked and swallowed hard. She would not cry. Not now in front of all these people. She was angry with herself. What a silly mistake. She knew the right answer so why had she given the wrong one? The boy in the seat next to her leaned forward. The teacher asked him the same question she had just asked Marcie. The boy answered it correctly. The audience clapped and cheered for him. He had won. "It just isn't fair," thought Marcie. She really knew, though, that it was fair. She had been too nervous and had answered without thinking carefully. She turned to the boy and shook his hand. "You did a good job," she told him. She was glad it was over. She knew that next year she would do even better.

1. How did Marcie feel in the beginning of the story?

_____

2. What clues tell you how she felt?

_____

3. What were Marcie, the boy, and the teacher doing?

_____

4. Who won?

_____

5. Was Marcie a good sport? Explain.

_____

_____

_____

6. What was Marcie planning at the end of the story?

_____

Picnic

Mother took out the bread, peanut butter, and jam. Brian and Kelsey made six sandwiches. They wrapped them in waxed paper. They put the sandwiches into the brown straw basket. Father filled a bottle with cold lemonade. "The sky is clear today," he smiled. "There won't be any rain to bother us!" Brian and Kelsey cut apples and carrots. They put the pieces into a plastic bag and added some grapes. Mother put a bag of cookies and some napkins into the basket. "The food is ready. Let's load the car," she said. Brian got the old blanket for sitting on the ground. He tossed it into the trunk. Kelsey gathered a few lawn games and some cards so they would have something to play. "We haven't done this in a long time," Kelsey laughed. "I hope the ants don't know we're coming!"

1. What is the family going to do?

_____

2. What clues tell you about what they are going to do?

_____

3. What are they taking to eat?

_____

4. Why did Brian bring the old blanket?

_____

5. Why was Father looking at the sky?

_____

6. What kind of sandwiches did they make?

_____

 CD-3710

Photograph

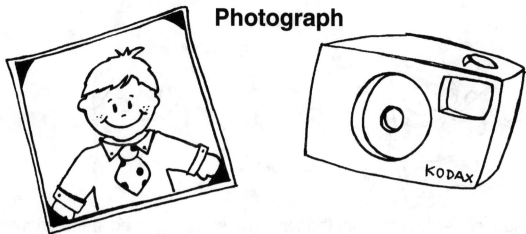

Jack was not comfortable. His new shirt was too stiff and his tie felt tight. Mother had fussed over his hair trying to get it to look just right. She made him scrub his hands three times to get all the dirt from under his fingernails! Finally his mom said he was ready. She smiled and said Jack looked very handsome in his suit. Jack frowned, but knew he could not tell his mom how he felt. This seemed to be very important to her. Jack sat on a special stool that turned and looked at the camera. He didn't feel like smiling at the lens, but he did his best. "Perfect!" smiled the man behind the camera as he snapped the shot. Jack posed two more times and then the man said they were finished. The first thing he did was take off his tie. Boy did that feel better!

1. What is Jack doing?

_____

2. What clues tell you where Jack is?

_____

3. How does Jack feel about this?

_____

4. What clues tell you how Jack feels?

_____

5. Who is the man that said "Perfect!"?

_____

6. Why did Jack take off his tie?

_____

Skiing

The hill looked really high from the top. The snow sparkled in the bright sun. It was pretty to look at, but Eric wasn't thinking about that. His stomach was fluttering and his hands began to sweat. He checked his boot straps. "See you at the bottom!" called Jessie. Eric watched as Jessie swished down the hill. Jessie was Eric's best friend, but at this moment Eric was not too happy with him. Jessie had talked Eric into trying this hill and now he was gone, leaving Eric by himself. Eric grasped the poles in his mittened hands. He hoped he would make it to the bottom without falling. This was the highest slope he had ever tried. "I can do this," he told himself firmly. Eric bent his knees and pushed off with the poles.

1. What is Eric doing?

_____

2. Which clues tell you?

_____

3. How does Eric feel about this?

_____

4. Why does he feel that way?

_____

5. Who is Jessie?

_____

6. Does Jessie feel the same way Eric does? Explain.

_____

_____

Blackie is Lost

    Kevin sat on his front porch. His head rested on his hands and his mouth was turned down at the corners. Where could Blackie be? Kevin had called and looked all over the neighborhood but couldn't find his friend. Kevin looked at the bone Blackie had left on the bottom step. Blackie always had that bone in her mouth. It was her favorite toy. Kevin did not know what to do. Blackie had been gone for four hours and could be miles away by now. Kevin heard a faint whine come from under the porch. He got down on his hands and knees and peered into the darkness. There was Blackie lying near the house! Her tail began to thump but she did not get up. Kevin saw something wiggling near Blackie's stomach. Puppies! Blackie had hidden to have her babies. Kevin laughed and went to get Mother.

1. How did Kevin feel at the beginning of the story?

_____

2. Which clues tell you how Kevin felt?

_____

3. Who is Blackie?

_____

4. What did Kevin think had happened to Blackie?

_____

5. What had really happened to Blackie?

_____

6. How do you think Kevin felt at the end of the story?

_____

A Visit to the City

Harry looked at his watch again. Time seems to go slowly when you are waiting. He picked up a newspaper and tried to read. The bustle of the station was too loud. He could not read here. Harry gave up trying and tossed the paper on the empty seat next to him. He hoped Kim would like the city. Harry had enjoyed visiting Kim's farm last summer. Now she was coming to see his city. Harry heard the whistle and the click-clack as the wheels rolled along the track. Kim was here! Harry waited as the passengers stepped down from the cars. Finally he saw Kim step down. "Welcome to Kingston!" he greeted her.

1. **Where was Harry waiting?**

_____

2. **Which clues tell you where he is?**

_____

3. **How did Harry feel as he waited?**

_____

4. **Which clues helped you figure out how he felt?**

_____

5. **Had Kim been to Kingston before?**

_____

6. **Where had Harry been last summer?**

_____

The Computer

John turned on the hard drive and watched the screen light up. He gathered his papers and began to type. The keyboard clacked as his fingers moved quickly over it. He had to get the letter printed before closing time. His boss had said the letter must be mailed today. John looked at the large clock over his desk. Would he finish in time? Soon the letter was typed. He ran the spelling program to see if there were any spelling errors. There were no mistakes! Just two minutes until closing time. John pressed the print button and watched as the letter magically appeared on the paper. He folded the letter, put it in an envelope, and put a stamp on the corner. He made it just in time!

1. What was John doing?

_____

2. Where is John?

_____

3. Which clues helped you decide where John is?

_____

4. What kind of machine is John using?

_____

5. What clues help tell you about the machine?

_____

6. How do you think John felt as he stamped the letter?

_____

Baking a Cake

Betty put the flour, eggs, sugar, and milk on the table. She got out her biggest bowl and mixing spoons. Her recipe was old, but she knew how great it tasted. Betty carefully measured the flour and sugar. She broke the eggs and added the milk. She stirred carefully and read the recipe often to be sure she was doing everything the right way. Betty mixed the batter until is was smooth. She poured it into a pan and popped it into the oven. Soon the warm smell of her baking filled the house. Oh, did it smell good! At the right time, Betty took the pan from the oven and set it near the window to cool. She would frost it and take it to the bake sale first thing tomorrow morning.

1. What was Betty doing?

_____

2. Which clues help you figure out what she is doing?

_____

3. What do you think Betty has made?

_____

4. Which clues help you figure out what Betty has made?

_____

5. What will Betty do with what she has made?

_____

6. When will she finish?

_____

Predicting

A.   Janice and Bill were going hiking. They had their lunches and water all packed and ready to go. Bill looked at the sky. The dark clouds were gathering and the wind was beginning to blow pretty hard.

1. What do you think Janice and Bill will do?

_____

2. Which clues helped you to decide?

_____

B.   Joey was busy playing basketball with his friends. His shoelace was untied but he didn't want to stop to tie it. Each time he ran, the lace bounced against the ground. Joey almost stepped on it six different times. Kyle passed the ball to Joey. Here was his big chance to score and win the game! Joey began to dribble toward the basket.

1. What do you think will happen?

_____

2. Which clues helped you to decide?

_____

C.   Mary awoke suddenly. Her room was very dark. She thought she heard a soft scratching sound at her window. There it was again! Mary's heart beat wildly. It might just be the tree branch rubbing against her window. It could also be something else. Mary had to find out. She reached for the light switch on the lamp by her bed.

1. What do you think Mary did?

_____

2. Which clues helped you to decide?

_____

Predicting

A.   Martin was riding his bike. He looked back to see if his friend was still behind him. Suddenly he heard the crunching of broken glass. Martin had ridden through the broken pieces of a bottle. His front tire began to wobble.

1. What do you think will happen?

_____

2. Which clues helped you to decide?

_____

B.   Sally sneezed again. She couldn't believe it. Today was the one day she could go to the circus and she was not feeling very well. Her face was hot and her throat was sore. "Did I hear you sneeze?" asked her mother. Sally had never lied to her mother, but she knew she could not go to the circus if Mom knew she was sick.

1. What do you think Sally will tell her mother?

_____

2. Which clues helped you to decide?

_____

C.   The children were playing baseball in the empty lot. Peggy was up to bat. She swung hard and hit the ball further than anyone else had. The ball sailed across the lot and smashed through Mrs. Allen's window. Mrs. Allen was always yelling at the children to go somewhere else to play. Peggy knew she would really be angry this time. The other kids scattered, running for home. Peggy stood in the field looking at the broken window.

1. What do you think Peggy will do?

_____

2. Which clues helped you to decide?

_____

Predicting

A.   Buddy was excited. His parents had said he could stay up as late as he wanted tonight. He had begged them for weeks to stay up and watch television. Now he could watch all those late night movies! Buddy was sure he could stay up until dawn. Shortly after ten o'clock Buddy began to yawn. "I am not tired!" Buddy told himself. By 10:30 his eyes began to grow heavy. Buddy shook himself to wake up.

1. What do you think will happen to Buddy?

_____

2. Which clues helped you to decide?

_____

B.   The spaceship landed on the planet Vexia. This planet was a "dead" planet with no life on it. The captain decided to go outside the ship and look around. As he stepped out the door, the captain saw something strange.

1. What do you think the captain saw?

_____

2. Which clues helped you to decide?

_____

C.   Andy had been told not to use his father's new telescope. But when he saw the puff of smoke over the woods behind the house, Andy knew he had to disobey. It had been a dry summer, and even a small fire in the woods would mean big trouble. Andy took the telescope to his treehouse and looked through it.

1. What do you think Andy saw?

_____

2. Which clues helped you to decide?

_____

Predicting

A.   John was in a hurry. He had a new kite and he wanted to try it out before dinner. It was a box kite. John had never put together a box kite before. "Dinner in ten minutes," called his mother. John tossed the directions into the trash. He did not have time to read them now. John quickly put the pieces together. There were two sticks left over so he jammed them into his pocket. He ran to the field to try out the new kite.

1. What do you think will happen with John's kite?

_____

2. Which clues helped you to decide?

_____

B.   Greg wanted to play ball, but not one of his friends were at the playground. The only boy around was Jerry, a new kid in school. Jerry was quiet and had not seemed too friendly during school. Greg was about to go home when he noticed that Jerry was holding a baseball mitt. Greg thought for a few minutes then walked over to Jerry.

1. What do you think Greg will do?

_____

2. Which clues helped you to decide?

_____

C.   Kristin was trying out for the lead in the school play. She wanted to learn the lines and do well at tryouts. Her friends, Sandy and Joan, wanted the same part. Every afternoon Sandy and Joan played at the park. They asked Kristin to play with them, but she went home and practiced her lines. On the day of tryouts, the three girls took turns saying the lines.

1. Who do you think got the part?

_____

2. Which clues helped you to decide?

_____

Predicting

A.   Kelly wasn't sure what she should do. She needed ten more dollars to buy the bike helmet she wanted. Now her friend Patty wanted to buy her old roller skates for twelve dollars. Kelly had gotten new skates for her birthday and she really didn't need the old ones. But her parents had told her she must check with them before she could sell or give away any of her things.

1. What do you think Kelly will do?

_____

2. Which clues helped you to decide?

_____

B.   The cold wind was blowing across town. Dark clouds gathered in the sky. The last few fall leaves danced on the wind as they let go of the bare tree limbs. Children hurried home to warm themselves. Their breath hung in little puffs in the air. The clouds grew darker and moved over the town.

1. What do you think will happen?

_____

2. Which clues helped you to decide?

_____

C.   Martha said she would help her neighbors while they were away. The neighbors said their plants needed a lot of water because they were about to bloom. Martha promised to water the garden every day while they were gone. The first day Martha watered all the plants. On the second day she forgot. It was such a warm day she stayed inside where it was cool. As a matter of fact, Martha forgot every day for a week.

1. What do you think happened to the garden?

_____

2. Which clues helped you to decide?

_____

Compound words are two words put together to make a new word. For example, snow and man can be put together to make the new word "snowman". Make sense out of the story below by putting the compound words in the blanks where they belong.

| backyard | campfire | fireflies | flashlight | lonesome |
| midnight | moonlight | rattlesnake | waterproof | weekend |

Camping

Last _____ I went camping.

I had a _____ tent in case it rained.

It was great fun at first. The _____

were glowing in the bushes. I built a warm _____.

The _____ was so bright I didn't even need my

_____! About _____ I

became _____ and a little scared. I thought I heard

a _____ near my tent. Thank goodness I was in my

own _____!

• •

| daylight | footprints | highway | lighthouse | rowboat |
| seashore | seaweed | sunlight | watermelon | grandmother |

At The Beach

Ryan awoke when it was almost _____. He got

dressed and called to his _____. They got into the

car and were soon on the _____ to the beach.

When they saw the tall _____ they knew they

were almost to the _____. Ryan ran across the

sand, leaving _____ as he ran. He played in the

bright _____ all day. He gathered

_____ and floated in a _____. For lunch

they had a cold _____ to cool them off.

Compound words are two words put together to make a new word. For example, snow and man can be put together to make the new word "snowman". Make sense out of the story below by putting the compound words in the blanks where they belong.

blackboard	breakfast	classroom	goodbye	homework
lunchroom	playground	schoolhouse	upstairs	windowsill

School

Caitlin likes to go to school. She eats _____, says

_____, and walks to school.

The_____ is two blocks from her house.

Caitlin's _____is _____on the

second floor. Her teacher writes the date on the

_____each day. Her desk is near the

window. If Caitlin leans on the _____she can see the

_____with the swings below. At noon the class

goes to the _____to eat. Caitlin enjoys the

_____she has to do every night!

• •

backyard	bathroom	bedroom	birdhouse	clubhouse
countryside	doorstep	fireplace	mailbox	neighborhood

At Home

I like my house. We live in a _____.

Our_____is in front of the house. There is a

_____in the big maple tree. I have a

_____in the _____. My

house has a large _____where D ad builds fires in the

winter. My _____is really nice. I even have my own

_____with a shower! I like to sit out front on the

_____because I can see the

whole_____from there.

         CD-3710

Name _____ skill: compound words

Compound words are two words put together to make a new word. For example, snow and man can be put together to make the new word "snowman". Make sense out of the story below by putting the compound words in the blanks where they belong.

baseball	basketball	driveway	dugout	football
inside	outdoors	quarterback	racetrack	touchdowns

Sports Crazy

Last week Evan went sports crazy! Monday he played flag
_____. He was the _____
and he made three _____. Tuesday he went to the
park to play _____. He hit a fly ball and got a home run!
His team in the _____went wild. Wednesday Evan
made a _____for his cars. Thursday it was too cold to play
_____so Evan played _____. On
Friday he shot baskets for three hours in his _____. He
said _____is his favorite sport of all.

• •

airplane	airport	afternoon	everywhere	headline
holdup	newspaper	policemen	Somebody	something

A Hero

Tyler was taking a trip. He went to the _____
but _____was wrong. Police cars were
_____. Three _____stood by
the front door. _____said there was a famous thief on
the _____. A man jumped from the plane and began to
run straight toward Tyler. Tyler stuck out his foot and tripped the man. Tyler
was a hero! That _____Tyler's picture was in the
_____. The _____said, "Tyler stops
a _____."

Compound words are two words put together to make a new word. For example, snow and man can be put together to make the new word "snowman". Make sense out of the story below by putting the compound words in the blanks where they belong.

| cowboy firefighter fisherman grownup mailman |
| policeman railroad somebody storyteller typewriter |

What Will I Be?

When I am a _____ I want to have a good job. I will

be a _____ and catch bad guys. I could also be a

_____ and drive a big red truck. I like to

work on the _____ so I could write books. I also like

trains. I could work on the _____. Dad says I am a

great _____ because I always catch the biggest fish.

But I like horses, so I might just be a _____. Maybe

I could be a _____ and deliver letters to far off places!

Mom says that _____ with my imagination would make a

good _____. What do you think I should be?

• •

| backpack blackberries blueberries butterflies daydream |
| footpath lunchtime nearby strawberries waterfall |

A Walk In The Woods

Mary likes to take walks in the woods. She fills her _____

with food to eat at _____. Along the path Mary finds

_____, _____, and

_____ to pick. She knows a small stream that has

a _____. She likes to sit near the splashing water

and _____ about her life. There are a lot of pretty

_____ that flit on the _____ flowers.

She follows the _____ home. What a wonderful way to

spend a day!

Name _____ Date _____

Compound words are two words put together to make a new word. For example, snow and man can be put together to make the new word "snowman". Make sense out of the story below by putting the compound words in the blanks where they belong.

candlelight   **dinnertime**   **earthquake**   **fireworks**   **housetop**
midnight   **rainstorm**   **thunder**   **thunderbolt**   **workmen**

The Storm

Last night, just before our _____, we had a terrible
storm. The _____was so loud it shook the house like a
little _____. The power went off and we had to eat dinner
by _____.The _____would not
quit. A large _____ struck our tree, knocking a branch into our
_____. The lightening was brighter than
_____in July! By _____
the rain began to stop. The next morning the yard was a mess.
_____had to clean up the broken tree
branches. What a storm!

lonesome   **anyone**   **homesick**   **rowboat**   **pancakes**
breakfast   **campfire**   **backward**   **anyone**   **into**

Away At Camp

Last summer I went away to camp for a week. At first I felt _____
because I didn't know _____ . The first night I was really
_____ . The next day things got better. We made
_____ to eat for _____ . We cooked them
over the _____ . Later we took a _____
across the lake. A boy named Jack stood up in the boat. He fell over _____
and went into the lake before _____could grab him. Jack wasn't
hurt. He was just wet. I helped Hack get back _____ the boat.
We became pals and I liked camp after that.

     78   CD-3710

Word Families

Fill in the blank with the word that makes sense in the sentence.

best   nest   pest   rest   test   west

1. Cowboys live out _____ .

2. A bug can be a _____ .

3. Baby birds live in a _____ .

4. I am tired so I will _____ now.

5. I think my drawing is the _____ one.

6. Today we had a _____ in math.

bet   get   let   net   Set   wet

1. I can _____ my own drink.

2. _____ the book down right here.

3. We used a _____ to catch the fish.

4. Joe got _____ in the rainstorm.

5. Please _____ me go to the show with you.

6. I _____ you cannot do that!

Word Families

Fill in the blank with the word that makes sense in the sentence.

bow	crow	know	show	slow	throw

1. A snail is a _____ animal.

2. I _____ the answer!

3. Betsy has a _____ in her hair.

4. John will _____ the ball to me.

5. Listen to that rooster _____ so early in the morning.

6. _____ me where you got hurt.

alive	arrive	chive	dive	five	hive

1. _____ pennies are the same amount as a nickel.

2. I will _____ at four o'clock.

3. Chris can _____ into the pool.

4. A tree is _____ but a rock is not.

5. Bees live in a _____ .

6. A _____ is a kind of onion.

Word Families

Fill in the blank with the word that makes sense in the sentence.

day	lay	May	play	say	way

1. This street goes only one _____ .

2. What did you _____ ?

3. I will _____ down and rest after my bath.

4. This has been a great _____ .

5. Will you _____ marbles with me?

6. _____ I have another cookie, please?

chip	clip	sip	slip	tip	whip

1. The _____ of my pencil is broken.

2. A lion tamer uses a _____ .

3. Do not _____ on that wet floor.

4. There is a _____ on the side of this glass.

5. May I have a _____ of water?

6. Mother will _____ the coupons from the paper.

Word Families

Fill in the blank with the word that makes sense in the sentence.

brain	chain	drain	pain	rain	stain

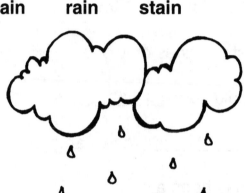

1. It looks like it might _____ today.

2. The dog is on a long _____ .

3. I have a _____ in my back.

4. The grape juice will _____ my shirt.

5. Let the water go down the _____ .

6. My _____ is not working well today!

check	deck	fleck	neck	peck	wreck

1. Wash the back of your _____ well.

2. Mom wrote a _____ to pay for the groceries.

3. I play with a _____ of cards.

4. There was a train _____ at the crossing last night.

5. The bird will _____ at the seeds.

6. I see a _____ of paint on the floor.

Word Families

Fill in the blank with the word that makes sense in the sentence.

age	cage	page	rage	stage	wage

1. Turn to _____ five in your history book.

2. The play will be on the big _____ in the auditorium.

3. My rabbit lives in a wire _____ .

4. The man flew into an angry _____ when we got away.

5. I am paid a _____ for the work I do.

6. This fossil is from the _____ of dinosaurs.

bump	dump	hump	jump	lump	stump

1. I have a _____ where the ball hit my head!

2. I did not mean to _____ into you.

3. Can you _____ rope with me today?

4. Please _____ the trash in the can.

5. Some whales have a _____ on their backs.

6. When they cut the tree down, only a _____ was left.

   CD-3710

Word Families

Fill in the blank with the word that makes sense in the sentence.

> **cream**   **dream**   **gleam**   **seam**   **stream**   **team**

1. The water is cold in that _____ .

2. I tore the _____ of my pants on the chair.

3. The child had a _____ in his eye when he understood.

4. At night I often _____ of nice things.

5. Please put _____ in my coffee.

6. I am on the baseball _____ .

> **delight**   **flight**   **light**   **might**   **night**   **right**

1. I need a _____ because it is dark in my room.

2. Owls stay awake all _____ .

3. It is a _____ to get a surprise!

4. Jason had his first _____ on an airplane.

5. I _____ go to the zoo tomorrow.

6. This answer is the _____ one.

 CD-3710

Word Families

Fill in the blank with the word that makes sense in the sentence.

brake   fake   lake   make   rake   stake

1. The diamond is a _____ !

2. I must _____ the car to a stop.

3. Hammer this tent _____ into the ground.

4. In fall, we _____ the leaves.

5. Can you _____ a snowman?

6. I would like to go swimming in the _____ .

behind   blind   find   kind   rind   wind

1. I must _____ my lost mitten.

2. Everyday we _____ the clock.

3. Put the lemon _____ in the trash.

4. I was _____ in the bright light.

5. I must hurry because I am _____ .

6. Be _____ to your friends.

 CD-3710

Word Families

Fill in the blank with the word that makes sense in the sentence.

ash   cash   lash   mash   rash   trash

1. Please _____ the potatoes.

2. I have a red _____ on my arms and face.

3. The fire left _____ everywhere!

4. I need _____ to buy this toy.

5. Put the _____ in the litter can.

6. My _____ fell on my cheek.

chop   crop   drop   mop   shop   stop

1. Do not _____ that glass because it will break.

2. I can _____ the floor tomorrow morning.

3. There is a _____ sign at the next corner.

4. We _____ in this store.

5. Corn is a good _____ to grow.

6. My dad will _____ the wood.

     86   CD-3710

Word Families

Fill in the blank with the word that makes sense in the sentence.

brace   face   grace   lace   pace   trace

1. There is _____ on my new dress.

2. I need a _____ for my broken arm.

3. Can you _____ the picture for me?

4. The horse has a fast _____ .

5. We say _____ before we eat our dinner.

6. The clown has a painted _____ .

bare   care   flare   glare   mare   share

1. I do not _____ for a drink now.

2. Mother can really _____ when she is angry.

3. The fire began to _____ hotly.

4. I have _____ legs when I wear shorts.

5. Will you _____ your lunch with me because I forgot mine?

6. That horse is a _____ .

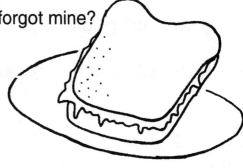

Word Families

Fill in the blank with the word that makes sense in the sentence.

camp	champ	Clamp	lamp	ramp	stamp

1. Put a _____ on the letter before you mail it.

2. _____ the two pieces of wood together so I can glue them.

3. He won so he is the new _____ .

4. I like to _____ in the woods.

5. I built a _____ for my skateboard jump.

6. This _____ gives off a lot of light.

back	rack	sack	snack	tack	track

1. The books are on a _____ by the front door of the library.

2. My _____ hurts from lifting too much at once.

3. After school, Kelly has a _____ because she is hungry.

4. I need a _____ to keep this poster on the bulletin board.

5. My race cars go on a _____ .

6. I put the groceries in a paper _____ .

Name _____

Here is a list of words. They all have something in common. What heading can you give this list that will name all the words? Write the heading on the line "Main Heading". Divide the list into two groups that are alike. Put the title of each group on the lines "Subheading" and fill in the box with the correct subheading words.

apple   banana   beans   blueberry   broccoli   carrot   celery   cherry
cucumber   grape   lemon   lettuce   lime   onion   orange   pea   peach
pear   plum   pumpkin   potato   raspberry   spinach   squash

Main Heading _____

Subheading:	**Subheading:**

Name _____ skill: classification

Here is a list of words. They all have something in common. What heading can you give this list that will name all the words? Write the heading on the line "Main Heading". Divide the list into two groups that are alike. Put the title of each group on the lines "Subheading" and fill in the box with the correct subheading words.

alone	awful	blue	cheerful	down	funny	gay	glad	glum
good	hurt	jolly	joyful	low	moody	pleased	proud	sad
	smiling	tearful	terrific	unhappy	unloved	wonderful		

Main Heading _____

Subheading:	Subheading:

Name _____ skill: classification

Here is a list of words. They all have something in common. What heading can you give this list that will name all the words? Write the heading on the line "Main Heading". Divide the list into two groups that are alike. Put the title of each group on the lines "Subheading" and fill in the box with the correct subheading words.

big	bitty	enormous	fat	giant	gigantic	great	huge
large	little	long	mammoth	miniature	petite	short	skinny
	slight	small	tall	teeny	thin	tiny	vast	wee

Main Heading _____

Subheading:	**Subheading:**

Here is a list of words. They all have something in common. What heading can you give this list that will name all the words? Write the heading on the line "Main Heading". Divide the list into two groups that are alike. Put the title of each group on the lines "Subheading" and fill in the box with the correct subheading words.

**draw   drew   hid   hide   jump   jumped   knew   know   sat
sit   stand   stood   swam   swim   tell   threw   throw   told
wake   win   woke   won   write   wrote**

Main Heading _____

Subheading:	Subheading:

Here is a list of words. They all have something in common. What heading can you give this list that will name all the words? Write the heading on the line "Main Heading". Divide the list into three groups that are alike. Put the title of each group on the lines "Subheading" and fill in the box with the correct subheading words.

**blizzard   bright   cloudless   cloudy   flurries   freeze   frozen
heat   hot   icy   pouring   puddles   sizzling   sleet
snow   snowflake   sprinkle   storm   sun   sunny
thunder   umbrella   warm   wet**

Main Heading _____

Subheading:	**Subheading:**	**Subheading:**

Name _____

Here is a list of words. They all have something in common. What heading can you give this list that will name all the words? Write the heading on the line "Main Heading". Divide the list into three groups that are alike. Put the title of each group on the lines "Subheading" and fill in the box with the correct subheading words.

**airplane   balloon   blimp   bus   canoe   car   jet
motorcycle   raft   rocket   rowboat   ship   space shuttle
submarine   train truck   tugboat   van**

Main Heading _____

Subheading:	**Subheading:**	**Subheading:**

Name _____

Here is a list of words. They all have something in common. What heading can you give this list that will name all the words? Write the heading on the line "Main Heading". Divide the list into three groups that are alike. Put the title of each group on the lines "Subheading" and fill in the box with the correct subheading words.

auditorium   cafeteria   cafeteria server   classroom   crayons
English   eraser   Gym   History   janitor   librarian   library   Math
nurse   office   pen   pencil   playground   principal   ruler
Science   scissors   Social Studies   teacher

Main Heading _____

Subheading:	Subheading:	Subheading:	Subheading:

        CD-3710

Homonyms are words that sound the same but are spelled differently and do not mean the same thing. Choose the correct homonym for each blank.

ant   aunt   ate   eight   eye   I

1. My mother's sister is my _____ .

2. There is an _____ hill in my front yard.

3. We _____ dinner last night.

4. I have _____ crayons in my box.

5. _____ want to play with you.

6. I have something in my _____ and it really hurts!

ad   add   be   bee   berry   bury

1. We put an _____ in the newspaper.

2. In math we _____ numbers together.

3. We will _____ leaving soon.

4. The _____ makes honey in its hive.

5. Pick that big _____ from the bush.

6. The dog will _____ a bone.

Name _____

Homonyms are words that sound the same but are spelled differently and do not mean the same thing. Choose the correct homonym for each blank.

blew   blue   brake   break   buy   by

1. The wind _____ last night.

2. I have _____ eyes.

3. The car _____ did not stop us in time.

4. The glass will _____ if you drop it.

5. May we _____ a new toy?

6. We walked _____ the library on our way home.

cent   scent   chews   choose   close   clothes

1. I have only one _____ in my bank.

2. The skunk has a strong _____ and it stinks.

3. The puppy _____ on my shoes.

4. Please _____ the one you like best.

5. You did not _____ the door tightly.

6. I wear warm _____ in winter.

                   CD-3710

Name _____

Homonyms are words that sound the same but are spelled differently and do not mean the same thing. Choose the correct homonym for each blank.

creak   creek   die   dye   fir   fur

1. Did you hear that _____ in the floor?

2. I had lunch beside the _____ in the woods.

3. The plant will _____ without water.

4. Mother will _____ my white pants blue.

5. A _____ tree is always green.

6. A bear has soft brown _____ .

flew   flu   flour   flower   new   knew

1. The birds _____ away when we came near.

2. Kathy is feeling ill with a case of the _____ .

3. Mother used _____ to make the bread.

4. The pink _____ smells so pretty!

5. I have _____ shoes.

6. Rick _____ the answer before I did.

         CD-3710

Homonyms are words that sound the same but are spelled differently and do not mean the same thing. Choose the correct homonym for each blank.

groan   grown   guessed   guest   hair   hare

1. Sue began to _____ when she hurt her arm.

2. The children have _____ this past year.

3. You are a _____ in our house.

4. We _____ the answer right away.

5. The man has a lot of _____ on his face.

6. Another name for a rabbit is _____ .

hear   here   high   hi   hole   whole

1. Can you _____ the music?

2. Put the chair right _____ on the rug, please.

3. The kite is _____ in the sky.

4. John is friendly and says _____ to everyone he meets.

5. The rabbit jumped down into a _____ under the bush.

6. We ate the _____ cake!

Name _____   skill: homonyms

Homonyms are words that sound the same but are spelled differently and do not mean the same thing. choose the correct homonym for each blank.

hour   our   knight   night   knot   not

1. Sixty minutes makes one _____.

2. That is _____ house.

3. The _____ lived in a castle.

4. Stars come out each _____ when the sun goes down.

5. My shoelace is in a _____ and I cannot untie it.

6. We will _____ go to the show tonight.

know   No   made   maid   mail   male

1. Do you _____ how to do this?

2. _____, I cannot do that right now.

3. We _____ a birdhouse to hang in the tree.

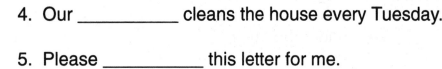

4. Our _____ cleans the house every Tuesday.

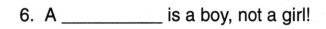

5. Please _____ this letter for me.

6. A _____ is a boy, not a girl!

Name _____

Homonyms are words that sound the same but are spelled differently and do not mean the same thing. Choose the correct homonym for each blank.

meat   Meet   missed   mist   oar   or

1. We get our _____ from different kinds of animals.

2. _____ me by the slide after school.

3. I _____ two days of school when I was sick.

4. The low cloud made a thick _____ over the land.

5. We row boats with a wooden _____ .

6. I will drink either milk _____ juice with my dinner.

one   won   pail   pale   pair   pear

1. I only had _____ piece of candy today.

2. Sally _____ the race because she finished first.

3. I carried water in the green _____ .

4. She looked _____ , as if she had seen a ghost.

5. I have a new _____ of purple socks.

6. We picked a _____ from the fruit tree.

Name _____

Homonyms are words that sound the same but are spelled differently and do not mean the same thing. Pick the correct homonym for each blank.

piece   peace   peal   Peel   plain   plane

1. I want a big _____ of cake.

2. I wish for _____ around the world.

3. The bells will _____ when I ring them!

4. _____ the apples and I will make a pie.

5. I like _____ white milk, with nothing in it.

6. We took a _____ to grandfather's house.

rain   reign   read   red   rose   rows

1. It looks as if it may _____ because there are black clouds.

2. The king will _____ for many years because he is only six years old.

3. I _____ a very good book last week.

4. Her face turned _____ because she was embarrassed.

5. Be careful of the thorns when you pick a _____.

6. The desks in our classroom are in neat little _____ .

102   **CD-3710**

Answer Key

Name _____   skill: comprehension

Christopher Columbus

Christopher Columbus was born in Italy in 1451. He did not have much education. He was an adult before he learned to read and write. Columbus planned to sail around the world to India, a country in eastern Asia. Queen Isabella of Spain gave him the ships Pinta, Nina, and Santa Maria. In 1492 Columbus and his men set sail. It took them about two months before they saw land again. Columbus was sure he had sailed around the world to India. He had really sailed across the Atlantic Ocean and landed on some islands near North America! Columbus found people on the islands and called them Indians. He made three more trips from Spain to these new islands. He mapped the way so that other people could follow the same route. Columbus died in 1506, still believing he had reached Asia.

1. **What is the main idea of this story?**
   a. It took two months to reach land.
   b. Columbus named the Indians.
   c. Columbus found a way to America.
2. **Where was Columbus born?**

   Italy

3. **Who gave the ships to Columbus?**

   Queen Isabella of Spain

4. **What were the names of the ships?**

   Nina, Pinta, Santa Maria

5. **Why did Columbus name the new people "Indians"?**

   He thought he had sailed to India

6. **How did Columbus help to develop North America?**

   He mapped the way so that others
   could follow the same route.

Think ahead: Look up Columbus in the encyclopedia. Find two new facts about him.

4   KW 1013

Name _____

Pocahontas

Pocahontas was an Indian Princess. Her father was the chief of a tribe. The tribe lived near Jamestown, an early English settlement in Virginia. Pocahontas was beautiful and very smart. In 1608 John Smith, a settler from Jamestown, was captured by the tribe. The Indians were going to kill him. Pocahontas saved his life. In 1613 Pocahontas was captured by the English. They taught her how they lived. She married a local farmer named John Rolfe. This helped the Indians and English become friends. Pocahontas and John had a son. She took the baby to England to visit. Pocahontas became very popular in England. She became ill and died there in 1617.

1. **What is the main idea of this story?**
   a. Pocahontas was an Indian.
   b. Pocahontas helped Indians and English become friends.
   c. Pocahontas died in England.
2. **What made Pocahontas a princess?**

   Her father was a chief.

3. **How did she help John Smith?**

   She saved his life

4. **What happened when the English captured her?**

   They taught her how they lived.

5. **How did her marriage help the Indians and the English?**

   It helped them become friends.

6. **How did Pocahontas help develop her country?**

   She helped bring the Indians and the
   English together

Think ahead: Look up Pocahontas in the encyclopedia. Find two new facts about her.

5   KW 1013

Name _____   skill: comprehension

John Cabot

John Cabot was born in Italy in 1451. He was a navigator, or sailor, and explorer. In 1497 King Henry VII of England hired John Cabot to find a way to the Orient (Japan and China). John crossed the Atlantic Ocean and landed in Canada. He called the area "New Found Land". The island he landed on is still called Newfoundland and is off the eastern coast of Canada. John Cabot explored this new land, looking for riches to take back to England. He sailed the coast as far south as Maine and north to Labrador, claiming the land for England. King Henry was pleased and sent Cabot on a second trip. Cabot was lost at sea in 1498 and was never seen again. The story of his first trip excited England and many other explorers came to Canada because of it.

1. **What is the main idea of this story?**
   a. John Cabot discovered Newfoundland.
   b. John Cabot was born in Italy.
   c. King Henry VII was pleased with John Cabot.
2. **In what year did Cabot land in Newfoundland?**

   1497

3. **Who hired Cabot to sail to the Orient?**

   King Henry VII of England

4. **Where is Newfoundland?**

   off the eastern coast of Canada.

5. **What happened on Cabot's second trip?**

   He was lost at sea

6. **How did Cabot help develop the New World?**

   He landed in Canada, named
   Newfoundland and explored the
   coast from Maine to Labrador.

Think ahead: Why is it hard to be the first person to explore a land no one knows about?

6   KW 1013

Name _____   skill: comprehension

Benito Juarez

Benito Juarez was a Zapotec Indian born in 1806. His parents died when he was only three. He lived in a small village and did not go to school when he was young. When Benito was 12 he moved to the city of Oaxaca to live with his sister. He went to school and learned to speak Spanish. He grew up, studied law, and became a judge. In 1852 he became the governor, or leader, of Oaxaca. The Spanish and French controlled much of Mexico at that time. Juarez began to fight for the rights of the Mexican people. He was exiled, or thrown out of the country, by President Santa Anna in 1853. He lived in New Orleans for two years and then returned to Mexico. Juarez was made President of Mexico in 1858. France invaded, or tried to take over, Mexico in 1862. Juarez lead his people in a fight against France and won. He remained President until he died in 1872.

1. **What is the main idea of this story?**
   a. Benito Juarez was an important Mexican leader.
   b. Benito Juarez was a Zapotec Indian.
   c. Juarez did not go to school until he was 12.
2. **What did Juarez study in school?**

   Spanish and law

3. **When was Juarez the governor of Oaxaca?**

   1852

4. **Where did Juarez live when he was exiled?**

   New Orleans

5. **When was Juarez made President of Mexico?**

   1858

6. **What did Juarez fight for?**

   The rights of the Mexican people

Think ahead: How was Benito Juarez important to the history of Mexico?

7   KW 1013

---

103   CD-3710

Answer Key

Name _____ skill: comprehension

Jacques Cartier

After John Cabot lead the way to North America many explorers followed him. Jacques Cartier, a French sailor, came to Canada in 1534. Cartier discovered the St. Lawrence River. He found land covered with huge forests and lakes. The forests were full of animals that could be used for fur. Cartier returned to France and told about the many beaver he had found. Beaver fur was popular in France so traders were interested in Canada. Cartier returned to the New World and became friends with the Indians. He understood the Indians so he did not try to take the land away. Instead of trapping the beavers, Cartier traded metal tools and cloth for the skins. The Indians were happy with Cartier and stayed friendly with the French for over 100 years.

1. **What is the main idea of this story?**
   a. Cartier was from France.
   (b.) Cartier found fur for France.
   c. Cartier became friends with the Indians.
2. **In what year did Cartier first come to Canada?**
   1534
3. **What did Cartier find in the New World?**
   Forests, lakes, beaver fur
4. **Why did the Indians like Cartier?**
   He did not want their land, they traded together
5. **Why were French traders interested in Canada?**
   beaver fur
6. **What river did Cartier explore?**
   St. Lawrence

Think ahead: What do you think might have happened if Cartier had taken the beaver rather than trading with the Indians?

©1995 Kelley Wingate Publications, Inc.   8   KW 1013

Name _____ skill: comprehension

Samuel de Champlain

France became interested in settling, or living in, the New World. In the early 1600's Samuel de Champlain came to North America to look for places where people could settle. Champlain explored the east coast of Canada and made the first map of the area. He explored and set up settlements in Nova Scotia and Maine. Champlain became friends with Huron Indians, helping them fight other Indian tribes. The Hurons helped him with fur trading and exploring. Champlain traveled down the St. Lawrence River and explored a beautiful lake which is now called Lake Champlain. The most important settlement Champlain began was called Quebec. Quebec became the capital of "New France", and is now the capital of the province of Quebec.

1. **What is the main idea of this story?**
   a. The Hurons liked Champlain.
   (b.) Champlain helped settle the eastern coast of Canada.
   c. A lake is named after Champlain.
2. **Why did Champlain come to the New World?**
   To look for places where people could settle.
3. **What area did Champlain explore?**
   the east coast of Canada
4. **How did Champlain help the Hurons?**
   He helped them fight other indian tribes.
5. **What is the name of the area Champlain helped settle?**
   Nova Scotia and Maine
6. **What was the most important settlement founded by Champlain?**
   Quebec

Think ahead: Find Lake Champlain on the map. What lands is it between?

©1995 Kelley Wingate Publications, Inc.   9   KW 1013

Name _____ skill: comprehension

Lewis and Clark

In the early 1800's most of the land west of the Mississippi River had not been explored. People wanted to find an easy way to cross the land and get to the Pacific Ocean. Two army officers, Merriweather Lewis and William Clark, were picked to find a way. They began their trip from St. Louis in 1804. They took boats up the Missouri River, but the trip was very long and hard. They kept records of everything they saw and did. They spent the winter in the Rocky Mountains with Indians The next spring an Indian woman named Sacajawea helped them to cross the mountains and go on to the ocean. They returned to St. Louis in 1806. Lewis and Clark had not found an easy route, but they had mapped the land. Now everyone knew what was between the Mississippi River and the Pacific Ocean.

1. **What is the main idea of this story?**
   a. Lewis and Clark were army officers.
   b. Sacajawea helped Lewis and Clark.
   (c.) Lewis and Clark explored and mapped the west.
2. **What did Lewis and Clark hope to find?**
   a way to the Pacific Ocean
3. **Who helped them get through the Rocky Mountains?**
   Sacajawea
4. **Where did their trip begin and end?**
   St. Louis
5. **How long did it take the men to get to the ocean and back?**
   Two years
6. **How did Lewis and Clark help to develop North America?**
   They mapped the land between the Mississippi River and the Pacific Ocean

Think ahead: Look up Lewis and Clark in the encyclopedia. Find two new facts about them.

©1995 Kelley Wingate Publications, Inc.   10   KW 1013

Name _____ skill: comprehension

Sitting Bull

The Sioux Indians were a tribe that lived in the Great Plains area. Sitting Bull was their leader for many years. He was loved by his people because he was brave, kind, and wise. He protected his tribe from other Indians and settlers. He wanted others to know that Indians were part of the country and had a right to their own land. In the 1870's gold was discovered on Sioux land. People wanted the gold so the army tried to take the land away. Sitting Bull helped defeat, or beat, the army in a famous battle at Little Bighorn. Then he led his people to Canada to keep them safe. Sitting Bull came back to the United States and was put in prison for two years. Then he was allowed to return to the Sioux reservation, a place set aside just for the Indians. He died in 1890 when some Indians killed him.

1. **What is the main idea of this story?**
   (a.) Sitting Bull was a great Sioux leader.
   b. He led his people to Canada.
   c. Sitting Bull helped at Little Bighorn.
2. **What tribe was Sitting Bull from?**
   Sioux
3. **Why was he so loved by his tribe?**
   He was brave, kind, and wise
4. **Why did the army want to take away the Sioux land?**
   Gold was discovered
5. **Where did he take his tribe to save them?**
   Canada
6. **How did Sitting Bull die?**
   He was killed by some Indians

Think ahead: Look up Sitting Bull in the encyclopedia. Find two new facts about him.

©1995 Kelley Wingate Publications, Inc.   11   KW 1013

Answer Key

Name _____   skill: comprehension

The Acadians

Many years ago the French had settled Acadia in Canada and the English had settled in the United States. England became interested in the northern land and wanted to settle there, too. In 1710 the two countries fought over Acadia and the English finally won. Acadia was renamed Nova Scotia. England said the French settlers could stay, but they had to be loyal, or faithful, to England. The Acadians did not want to do that so the English made them leave in 1755. The French Acadians were put on ships and sent to settle south, in the United States. The ships were very small so the Acadians could not take much with them. They were scattered, or spread out, in the United States. Many families were parted and never saw each other again. Some of the Acadians found their way to a French settlement in Louisiana. They settled there and became known as the Cajun people. Many Cajuns still live in southern Louisiana.

1. **What is the main idea of this story?**
   a. The English and French fought over Acadia.
   b. England won Acadia.
   c. French Acadians were moved to the United States.
2. **In what year did England win Acadia?**

   1710
3. **Why were the French Acadians moved?**

   They would not be loyal to England.
4. **Where were the Acadians sent?**

   to the United States
5. **Why did the Acadians move to Louisiana?**

   There were French people there.

6. **What are the Acadians called today?**

   Cajuns

Think ahead: Why do you think the French Acadians moved instead of becoming part of England?

©1995 Kelley Wingate Publications, Inc.   12   KW 1013

Name _____   skill: comprehension

Harriet Tubman

Harriet Tubman was a slave. As a young girl she dreamed of freedom for her people. In 1849 Harriet escaped. She followed the north star until she was safe in New York. For the next ten years Harriet made many trips back south. She helped hundreds of slaves escape, including her own parents. They used the Underground Railroad, a secret group of people who helped slaves pass safely to the north. When the Civil War began, Harriet helped the northern army. She cooked, helped nurse the wounded, and even spied for the army. When she died in 1913, Harriet was buried with full army honors.

1. **What is the main idea of this story?**
   a. Harriet was a spy.
   b. Harriet helped many slaves find freedom.
   c. Harriet was a slave.
2. **How did Harriet escape?**

   She followed the north star to New York
3. **What was the Underground Railroad?**
   a. A railroad that carried slaves.
   b. A group that helped slaves escape to the north.
   c. A tunnel to the north.
4. **How did Harriet help during the Civil War?**

   She cooked, help nurse the wounded,
   and even spied.
5. **How was Harriet honored when she died?**

   She was buried with full army honors
6. **How did Harriet Tubman help people?**

   She helped slaves become free.

Think ahead: Look up Harriet Tubman in the encyclopedia. Find two new facts about her.

©1995 Kelley Wingate Publications, Inc.   13   KW 1013

Name _____   skill: comprehension

Clara Barton

Clara Barton was born in 1812. She was a school teacher for many years. She was over forty years old when the Civil War began. Clara helped care for the wounded soldiers. She helped set up hospitals near the battlefields. Clara worked hard to see that they had bandages, drugs, and other needed supplies. Soon she was known as "The Angel of the Battlefield". When she was fifty, Clara went to Europe to help in another war. While there she learned about the Red Cross, a group that helps take care of people during a war. Clara returned to the United States and started the American Red Cross. She became the first American Red Cross president in 1881, when she was almost sixty years old.

1. **What is the main idea of this story?**
   a. Clara Barton was a school teacher.
   b. Clara Barton was "The Angel of the Battlefield".
   c. Clara Barton helped during wars.
2. **What was Clara's first job?**

   She was a school teacher.
3. **How did Clara help the wounded during the Civil War?**

   She helped set up battlefields near
   the hospital.
4. **What was Clara's nickname?**

   "the angel of the battlefield"
5. **Where did she learn about the Red Cross?**

   Europe
6. **How did Clara Barton help people?**

   She helped take care of wounded
   soldiers. She started the American
   Red Cross.

Think ahead: Look up Clara Barton in the encyclopedia. Find two new facts about her.

©1995 Kelley Wingate Publications, Inc.   14   KW 1013

Name _____   skill: comprehension

The Wright Brothers

Orville and Wilbur Wright were famous American brothers. They owned a bicycle shop in Dayton, Ohio. Although they were interested in bicycles, they also loved the idea of flying. In 1896 they began to experiment, or try new ideas, with flight. They started by testing kites and then gliders, which are motorless planes. These tests taught them how an airplane should rise, turn, and come back to earth. The brothers made over 700 glider flights at Kitty Hawk, a field in North Carolina. This was fun, but not good enough for them. Orville and Wilbur put a small engine on a plane they named Flyer I. On December 17, 1903 they took the first motor-powered flight that lasted about one minute. They continued to experiment until they could stay in the air for over one hour.

1. **What is the main idea of this story?**
   a. Testing new ideas is important.
   b. Flyer I was the first airplane.
   c. The Wright brothers were early pilots.
2. **What does the word "experiment" mean?**
   a. to try new ideas
   b. to test kites
   c. to stay in the air for one hour
3. **Where did the brothers test their gliders and plane?**

   Kitty Hawk, North Carolina
4. **How long did the first motor-powered flight last?**

   about one minute
5. **How did the brothers learn about what makes planes work?**

   They flew kites and gliders.
6. **How did the Wright brothers help people?**

   They learned how to make
   and fly airplanes.

Think ahead: Look up the Wright brothers in the encyclopedia. Find two new facts about them.

©1995 Kelley Wingate Publications, Inc.   15   KW 1013

Answer Key

Name _____ skill: comprehension

Amelia Earhart

Amelia Earhart was a famous woman pilot. She loved to fly planes. She was an early pioneer in American flight. In 1932 Amelia was the first person to fly alone from Newfoundland to Ireland. In 1935 she flew across the Pacific Ocean from Hawaii to California. In 1937 Amelia and her copilot, F.J. Noonan, tried to fly the equator all the way around the world. Their plane was lost and never found again. No one knows what happened to them. Some people think the plane crashed into the ocean. Others believe Amelia and Noonan were captured by the Japanese and that she is still alive today. Her last flight has been a famous mystery for over fifty years.

1. **What is the main idea of this story?**
   a. Amelia Earhart was a famous pilot.
   b. Amelia Earhart disappeared.
   c. Amelia Earhart was lost at sea.
2. **Who was Amelia Earhart?**

   a pilot and pioneer in flight
3. **Why was her 1932 flight so important?**

   She was the first person to fly alone from Newfoundland to Ireland.
4. **When did she fly from Hawaii to California?**

   1935
5. **What two things do people believe might have happened to Amelia and Noonan?**

   Their plane may have crashed into the ocean. They may have been captured by the Japanese.

Think ahead: Look up Amelia Earhart in the encyclopedia. Find two new facts about her.

©1995 Kelley Wingate Publications, Inc.   16   KW 1013

Name _____ skill: comprehension

Thomas Edison

Thomas Alva Edison spent the first part of his life in Port Huron, Michigan. When he was in sixth grade his teacher said he was addled, not very smart, and so he quit school. Tom began to work selling newspapers and candy on a local railroad. He liked to experiment and spent all of his money on books and chemicals for his labratory. When he was about eighteen he invented the automatic telegraph, a machine that sends messages. He began to invent other things and opened a business in New Jersey. Soon he had many people working on his ideas. In 1879 Edison invented the first light bulb, a safer way to light homes and businesses. He later invented the phonograph, batteries, and the movie projector. By the time he died in 1931, Thomas Edison had over 1,000 inventions!

1. **What is the main idea of this story?**
   a. Thomas Edison quit school in the sixth grade.
   b. Edison invented the light bulb.
   c. Thomas Edison was a great inventor.
2. **What does the word "addled" mean?**
   a. very smart
   b. not very smart
   c. a machine to send messages
3. **What was Edison's first invention?**

   The automatic telegraph
4. **Name three other Edison inventions.**

   light bulb, phonograph, batteries, movie projector
5. **How did Thomas Edison help people?**

   He invented many things that people use.

Think ahead: Look up Thomas Edison in the encyclopedia. Find two new facts about him.

©1995 Kelley Wingate Publications, Inc.   17   KW 1013

Name _____ skill: comprehension

Henry Ford

Henry Ford was born in 1863 near Dearborn, Michigan. As a young boy he liked machines, and in 1890 he began to experiment with horseless carriages—the first cars. He built his first car in 1896. Each car had to be made by hand, so cars were difficult to build and cost a lot of money. Henry Ford figured out a way to make many cars at once. His invention became known as the assembly line. All the car parts were made and brought to a large, rolling belt. The parts were added on one piece at a time as the car rolled by on the belt. This process made cars easier to build and cost less money. Later on Henry designed the Model T Ford, which was a very popular car for many years.

1. **What is the main idea of this story?**
   a. Henry Ford made it easier to build cars.
   b. Henry Ford invented the first car.
   c. Henry Ford made the Model T.
2. **Where was Ford born?**

   Michigan
3. **What made him famous?**

   He invented the assembly line.
4. **What was the horseless carriage?**
   a. an assembly line
   b. a car
   c. a rolling belt
5. **How did the assembly line work?**

   Car parts were put together as cars rolled by
6. **How did Henry Ford help people?**

   He made cars easier to make and less expensive.

Think ahead: Look up Henry Ford in the encyclopedia. Find two new facts about him.

©1995 Kelley Wingate Publications, Inc.   **18**   KW 1013

Name _____ skill: comprehension

Earth and Sun

The earth is a large round planet that circles around the sun. The top of the earth is the north pole and the bottom is the south pole. A pretend line called an axis is the line that goes from the north pole through the earth to the south pole. The earth spins on this axis. Put a stick through the middle of an apple and turn it. That is just like the earth's axis. The axis does not go straight up and down. It is tilted, or turned a little to one side. As the earth goes around the sun, sometimes the north pole is closer to the sun than the south pole. Then it is summer in the north and winter in the south. When the earth gets to the other side of the sun, the south pole is closer and has summer while the north pole has winter. This is how the earth gets seasons.

1. **What is the main idea of this story?**
   a. How the earth's tilt and the sun give us seasons.
   b. The earth spins on an axis.
   c. Winter comes once a year.
2. **What is an axis?**

   A line that goes from the North pole through the earth to the Southpole
3. **When a pole is closest to the sun, what season is it?**

   summer
4. **When a pole is farthest from the sun, what season is it?**

   winter
5. **What is a word that means "turned to one side"?**
   a. axis
   b. tilted
   c. pole
6. **Why is it summer when we are nearer the sun?**

   because we are closer to the heat and light of the sun.

Think ahead: What happens when both poles are the same distance from the sun?

©1995 Kelley Wingate Publications, Inc.   19   KW 1013

Answer Key

Name _____   skill: comprehension

Summer

When the earth is tilted toward the sun we have a warm season or time of year that we call summer. During the summer it feels warmer because we are closer to the sun. Warm weather is a good time for plants to grow. They use the sun to make food and grow bigger. During the summer people wear lighter clothes to stay cool. They wear hats and sunglasses to protect themselves from the hot sun because it is easier to get sunburned during this hot season. We have more hours of sunlight and less hours of darkness during the summer. The longer days let us stay up later and enjoy the outdoors more.

1. **What is the main idea of this story?**
   a. Summers are hot.
   b. Wear hats to protect yourself from the sun.
   c. Summer is a season when we are closer to the sun.
2. **What does the word "season" mean?**
   a. warmer weather
   b. a time of year
   c. closer to the sun
3. **Why is the summer warmer than other seasons?**
   Because we are closer to the sun.
4. **Why do plants grow well during the summer?**
   Because it is warmer.
5. **Why should people protect themselves from the sun?**
   Because it is easy to get sunburned
6. **Are summer days longer or shorter? Why?**
   Summer days are longer. Because the earth is tilted toward the sun and we are closer to the sun.

Think ahead: Tell what you like to do during the summer season.

©1995 Kelley Wingate Publications, Inc.   20   KW 1013

Name _____   skill: comprehension

Plants

Plants eat and grow. They are living things. A plant has three main parts: roots, a stem, and leaves. Each part does an important job to keep the plant alive. The roots are the part of a plant that stays in the ground. Roots take in water and nutrients from the soil. The water and nutrients are what a plant uses for food. Roots also hold the plant up, keeping it from falling over. The stem of a plant is the main trunk. This part has the veins, or tubes, that carry food from the roots to the leaves. The leaves gather energy from the sun to help turn the nutrients into food. Leaves also take in carbon dioxide, a gas that plants breathe. Every plant also makes seeds so new plants can grow. Seeds of plants can be the nut, flower, vegetable, or fruit that grows on the plant.

1. **What is the main idea of this story?**
   a. Plants have veins.
   b. Plants get water through their roots.
   c. Plants have three main parts.
2. **What are the three main parts of a plant?**
   roots, stem, leaves
3. **What does each part do that helps keep the plant alive?**
   a. roots take in water and nutrients
   b. stems carry food from roots to leaves
   c. leaves gather energy and take in
4. **What is another name for nutrients?**
   food
5. **What is carbon dioxide?**
   a gas that plants breathe

Think ahead: Draw a picture of your favorite plant. Label the roots, stem, and leaves.

©1995 Kelley Wingate Publications, Inc.   21   KW 1013

Name _____   skill: comprehension

Fall

After summer comes the fall season. During this time of year our part of the world gets ready for winter. The weather becomes cooler. Leaves fall from the trees. The fruit, vegetables, and nuts of trees and plants are ripe and ready to pick. Animals gather seeds and nuts to store for the winter. Their fur grows longer and thicker to protect them from the cold. Some birds fly south to find warmer weather. People also gather food and store much of it for the winter. They get out sweaters and jackets to keep themselves warm as the weather becomes cooler. The hours of day and night are about equal during this season because we are moving away from the sun.

1. **What is the main idea of this story?**
   a. Animals prepare for colder weather.
   b. Fall is a cool season.
   c. People gather food for the winter.
2. **What happens to the weather in the fall?**
   the weather becomes cooler
3. **What do animals do in the fall?**
   They gather seeds and nuts.
4. **How do people prepare for the fall?**
   They gather food and store it.
5. **What happens to the days and nights?**
   They become about equal it length.
6. **Why isn't the fall weather very hot or very cold?**
   Because we are between being close to the sun and being far away from the sun.

Think ahead: Tell about some changes in plants you might have noticed in the fall.

©1995 Kelley Wingate Publications, Inc.   22   KW 1013

Name _____   skill: comprehension

Acorns

Oak trees grow nuts called acorns. These nuts are really the seeds of the oak tree. In the fall the acorns are ripe. Squirrels love to eat the acorns. They carry the nuts to their nests to eat. Squirrels also bury some acorns to save them for the winter. Sometimes the squirrels cannot remember where they buried the acorns. The nut stays in the ground all winter. In the spring the warm rain softens the shell and the acorn begins to grow. If nothing disturbs the new plant it will grow into a new oak tree.

1. **What is the main idea of this story?**
   a. Acorns are the seeds of oak trees.
   b. Squirrels love acorns.
   c. Spring rains make acorns grow.
2. **An acorn is:**
   a. the branch of an oak tree
   b. the seed of an oak tree
   c. a squirrels nest
3. **How do acorns get into the ground?**
   Squirrels bury them.
4. **What are two uses for acorns?**
   Food for squirrels and to grow a new plant.
5. **Why do squirrels bury acorns?**
   To save them for winter food
6. **What happens if the buried acorn is not disturbed?**
   The warm spring rain softens the shell and the acorns begin to grow.

Think ahead: Draw a picture of an acorn on an oak tree.

©1995 Kelley Wingate Publications, Inc.   23   KW 1013

Answer Key

Name _____ skill: comprehension

Deciduous Trees

When fall comes the leaves of some trees change color and then fall to the ground. Trees that lose their leaves are called deciduous. Why do the leaves fall? A tree has veins, or tubes, like humans do. A tree's veins are filled with sap instead of blood. The sap carries water and minerals from the roots to the leaves. If the sap were to stay in the branches all winter, it may freeze and the tree would die. Instead, the sap goes down into the roots where it will be warmer during the winter. Without sap the leaves cannot live, so they dry up and fall off. In the spring the sap goes back up to the branches and the tree grows new leaves.

1. **What is the main idea of this story?**
   a. Sap goes to the roots.
   b. Trees that lose their leaves are deciduous.
   c. Leaves dry up and fall off the trees.
2. **Deciduous means:**
   a. Trees that lose their leaves
   b. branches without sap
   c. veins
3. **What does a tree have that is like our blood?**

   sap
4. **Where does sap go for the winter? Why?**

   Into the roots to stay warm
5. **Another word for vein is:**
   a. sap
   b. deciduous
   c. tube
6. **When does a deciduous tree grow new leaves?**

   In the spring time when it begins to get warm.

Think ahead: Draw a picture of a summer leaf and a fall leaf.

©1995 Kelley Wingate Publications, Inc.   24   KW 1013

Name _____ skill: comprehension

Winter

Winter is the season when your part of the earth is tilted away from the sun. The sun cannot warm the earth as well because it is further away. The air is much colder during this season. Many plants and animals protect themselves from the cold. Some plants push their sap into their roots and stop growing. Some animals hibernate, or go to sleep, in warm holes all winter. People heat their houses to stay warm. When they go outside they wear coats, mittens, and hats to protect them from the cold. Water from the clouds freezes and falls as snow. It covers the ground in a cold white blanket for the winter.

1. **What is the main idea of this story?**
   a. Winter is a cold season.
   b. Some animals hibernate.
   c. Snow covers the ground in winter.
2. **Why does the air get colder in winter?**

   Because we are tilted away from the sun
3. **How do plants protect themselves in winter?**

   They push their sap into their roots and stop growing.
4. **A word that means "to sleep all winter" is:**
   a. tilted
   b. hibernate
   c. protect
5. **How do people protect themselves in winter?**

   They wear coats, hats and mittens.
6. **Why does it snow in winter?**

   Because water from the clouds freezes and falls as snow.

Think ahead: Draw a picture of what you like to do during the winter season.

©1995 Kelley Wingate Publications, Inc.   25   KW 1013

Name _____ skill: comprehension

Snow

Snow is a form of water that falls from clouds during very cold weather. The cloud temperature must be freezing to make snow. Water vapor is frozen into tiny ice crystals in the cold air. The crystals join together to form a snowflake. Each snowflake has its own shape. No two are alike! The cold air keeps the snowflake from melting as it falls. The first snow of the season quickly melts, turns back into water, when it lands on the ground. That is because the ground is still warm from the summer and fall seasons. As more snow falls, it cools the earth and even freezes the top few inches. Now the snow will stay and build up until the sun is warm enough to melt it.

1. **What is the main idea of this story?**
   a. Snow is a crystal.
   b. Snow is very cold.
   c. How snow is made.
2. **What is snow?**

   a form of water
3. **How does water change into snow?**

   It is frozen into ice crystals.
4. **A word that means "to change water into ice" is:**
   a. melt
   b. freeze
   c. snow
5. **What does the word "melt" mean?**

   Turns back into water
6. **Why does the first snow melt on the ground?**

   Because the ground is still warm from the summer and fall seasons.

Make a snowflake: Fold a piece of paper into a small square and cut shapes from the sides. Open it upto see your snowflake.

©1995 Kelley Wingate Publications, Inc.   26   KW 1013

Name _____ skill: comprehension

Spring

Spring is the season that comes after winter and before summer. Your part of the earth is turning back toward the sun. The snow melts and the air begins to warm again. Sap slowly climbs back into the trunk and branches of trees. New leaves begin to grow on plants. The ground thaws as it is warmed by the sun and melting snow. Animals come out of hibernation and look for food to eat. Spring brings a lot of rain that helps warm the earth. People take out umbrellas and put away their heavy winter clothes. The earth seems to wake up and begin to grow once again.

1. **What is the main idea of this story?**
   a. Spring warms the earth so things can grow.
   b. Snow melts in the spring.
   c. New leaves grow on plants.
2. **What is spring?**

   The season after winter and before summer.
3. **How do the plants wake up?**

   The sap climbs into the trunk and branches.
4. **A word that means "thaw" is:**
   a. rain
   b. unfreeze
   c. snow
5. **Why does your part of the earth begin to warm in the spring?**

   Because it tilts toward the sun.
6. **Why do people need umbrellas in the spring?**

   Because there is a lot of rain.

Think ahead: Tell how the sun affects the earth for each of the four seasons.

©1995 Kelley Wingate Publications, Inc.   27   KW 1013

Answer Key

Water Cycle

After a rainstorm you see a lot of puddles. The sun shines and the wind blows. Soon the puddles are gone. The sun and wind have turned the water into a gas called water vapor. This change from liquid to gas is called evaporation. As the water vapor rises with the air it sticks to small pieces of dust. As the air gets cooler the vapor changes back to water. This is called condensation. The dust and condensation gather together to form clouds. When there is too much water for the cloud to hold, the water falls back to the earth as precipitation, like rain or snow. This process of evaporation, condensation, and precipitation is called a water cycle.

1. What is the main idea of this story?
   a. How a water cycle works.
   b. Water can evaporate.
   c. Rain and snow are precipitation.
2. How does water vapor get into the air?
   The sun and wind evaporate the water.
3. What is condensation?
   Water vapor changing into water
4. How does water vapor turn back into water?
   It becomes cooler and condenses
5. What is a cloud?
   Dust and water vapor
6. What word means both rain and snow?
   Precipitation

Think ahead: Draw a picture that shows how a water cycle works.
©1995 Kelley Wingate Publications, Inc.   28   KW 1013

Clouds

Evaporated water, also called water vapor, rises in the air. Air high above the ground is cooler than the air near the ground. When the water vapor meets the cooler air it condenses, changes back to water, on small pieces of dust. Each tiny piece of dust with water is called a droplet. A cloud is made of billions of droplets. There are many kinds of clouds. Some clouds form near the ground. These clouds are called fog and they make it hard to see very far. Some clouds are large and fluffy. They look like cotton balls in the sky. When a cloud gathers more water droplets than it can hold it becomes dark and is called a storm cloud. Some clouds are very high in the sky and look like feathers. These clouds are made of frozen water vapor, or tiny pieces of ice. Each type of cloud looks different, but they are all made from water vapor and dust.

1. What is the main idea of this story?
   a. A cloud is made of water droplets.
   b. Fog is a kind of cloud.
   c. There are many kinds of clouds.
2. What is a cloud?
   A cloud is made of billions of tiny droplets.
3. What is a storm cloud?
   a cloud that has more water droplets than it can hold
4. What do you call a cloud that is near the ground?
   fog
5. What are high feathery clouds made of?
   frozen water vapor, tiny pieces of dust
6. How do clouds help the earth?
   they give us rain

Think ahead: Draw a picture of the clouds you can see today.
©1995 Kelley Wingate Publications, Inc.   29   KW 1013

Precipitation

Water that falls to the earth is called precipitation. Not all precipitation is rain. If the raindrops fall through air that is freezing, they will freeze and become sleet. When the temperature of the cloud is freezing the water droplets may form into tiny ice crystals. The crystals join together to make snowflakes. If the snowflakes fall through air that is also freezing, we will get snow. If the cloud droplets freeze into large balls of ice we may get hail. Rain, sleet, snow, and hail are all forms of precipitation.

1. What is the main idea of this story?
   a. There are ice crystals in clouds.
   b. There are different kinds of precipitation.
   c. Hail and snow are precipitation.
2. Name four types of precipitation.
   rain   snow
   sleet   hail
3. What is the cloud temperature when it snows?
   freezing
4. What is the air temperature when it sleets or snows?
   freezing
5. What is the temperature of the air and cloud when it rains?
   warm
6. What is hail?
   cloud droplets that freeze into large balls of ice

Think ahead: Draw the four types of precipitation.
©1995 Kelley Wingate Publications, Inc.   30   KW 1013

Living Things

Some things are alive and some are not. A tree is alive. A rock is not alive. A robot can move and even talk, but it is not alive. How are living things different from things that are not alive? Here is how:
1. Living things can grow and change. An acorn grows into an oak tree. A baby grows into an adult.
2. All living things need energy. Energy is the ability to do work. Living things get energy from their food.
3. All living things can reproduce, or make new living things. A plant drops seeds so new plants will grow. Animals have babies or lay eggs.

1. What is the main idea of this story?
   a. Living things grow, need energy, and reproduce.
   b. Robots are not living things.
   c. Some things are alive and some are not.
2. What are three features that make living things different from things that are not alive?
   they grow   they reproduce
   they need energy
3. What word means "to make new living things"?
   a. energy
   b. reproduce
   c. alive
4. A robot uses energy. Why isn't it alive?
   It does not grow. It does not reproduce
5. A cloud can grow and change. Why isn't it alive?
   It does not reproduce

Think ahead: Make a list of six things that are alive and six things that are not alive.
©1995 Kelley Wingate Publications, Inc.   31   KW 1013

Answer Key

Name _____   skill: comprehension

Energy

Whenever something moves or changes, energy is being used. When wood burns or water turns to ice, it takes energy. Energy means being able to do work. There are different forms of energy. One form is heat energy. If you put a pot of water on a heated stove, when it is hot enough, the water will begin to boil. When you take the heat away the water cools and stops boiling. Light is an important form of energy. Plants use light to grow. We use light to see. Without light we could not live. Another form of energy is sound. Sounds are caused by things that vibrate, or move quickly back and forth. A drum vibrates when it is hit. The vibrations reach your ears and you hear the sound. Much of the energy we use is stored in other things. The food we eat has stored energy that helps us to walk, talk, and live. Energy is what makes the world move!

1. **What is the main idea of this story?**
   a. Energy is used to change or move things. *(circled)*
   b. Light is energy.
   c. Energy can be stored.
2. **Where do plants get most of their energy?**
   light
3. **When a piano is played, what kind of energy does it make?**
   sound
4. **What are the kinds of energy this story talks about?**
   heat, light, sound
5. **What is energy used for?**
   To move or change things

Think ahead: Make a list of four things that use energy and four things that make energy.

Name _____   skill: comprehension

The Sun

At night the sky is full of stars. Stars are burning balls of gases that give off heat and light energy. The stars look small and we cannot feel any of their heat because they are so far away. One star that we can see and feel the heat from is our sun. We are close enough to have the heat energy from the sun warm our earth. The sun's light makes our days bright and gives plants energy to grow. The sun is the most important star for the earth. If it were too far away the earth would grow cold and plants would die. If the sun were too close to the earth it would be so hot that things would burn and die. It is nice that our star is right where it is!

1. **What is the main idea of this story?**
   a. The sun is a star. *(circled)*
   b. Earth is too far from other stars.
   c. We can see and feel the sun.
2. **What is a star?**
   a burning ball of gas
3. **Why can't we feel the heat from other stars?**
   they are too far away
4. **What kinds of energy do we get from the sun?**
   heat and light
5. **What would happen if the sun were closer or further from the earth?**
   we would be too hot or too cold
6. **Why is the sun so important to the earth?**
   It gives us heat and light.

Think ahead: What might happen to the earth if the sun ever burns out?

Name _____   skill: comprehension

Climate

The climate of an area is the usual weather it has over a long time. North America has very different climates from area to area. The northern states are closer to the north pole than the equator. They have mild summers (not harsh or too warm) and long winters that are filled with ice and snow. The southern areas have long hot summers and mild winters because they are closer to the equator. The southwestern areas have a dry climate. They do not get a lot of rainfall. Both the eastern and western coasts have heavy rainfall. The climate of an area affects, or changes, how people live. It helps us decide what kind of houses to live in or what type of clothes to wear.

1. **The main idea of this story is:**
   a. Many areas have mild winters.
   b. Climate affects the way we live.
   c. Climate is the weather an area has during the year. *(circled)*
2. **Why do the northern parts of North America have long winters?**
   because they are closer to the north pole.
3. **Why do the southern parts of North America have long summers?**
   because they are closer to the equator
4. **What does the word "mild" mean?**
   a. gentle, not harsh *(circled)*
   b. hot
   c. dry
5. **Which area has a dry climate?**
   the southeastern area
6. **How does the climate affect the way we live?**
   It helps us decide what kind of houses to live In or what type of clothes to wear.

Think ahead: What kind of climate do you live in? How does it affect you?

Name _____   skill: comprehension

Making a Living

The kind of climate we live in can affect how we make a living. In some parts of the country the weather makes the soil, or dirt, good for certain growing crops. In other areas it is difficult to grow much of anything. The low, wet lands may be good for crops such as rice or sugar cane. Drier land is good for corn or wheat. Grasslands are best for raising cattle or sheep. People who live in dry desert areas will not be able to grow fields of crops. They will have to make their living some other way. Some mountain areas are good for crops like tobacco but not rice or wheat. Other mountain areas are best for mining coal or other minerals. Where you live may affect the type of job you do.

1. **The main idea of this story is:**
   a. Some soil is good for growing crops.
   b. Climate may affect how we make a living. *(circled)*
   c. Mining is done in the mountain areas.
2. **What crops grow well in low, wet areas?**
   rice or sugar
3. **What type of area would you live in to raise cows?**
   grasslands
4. **What does the word "soil" mean?**
   a. climate
   b. metal
   c. dirt *(circled)*
5. **Where might you live if you were a miner?**
   in the mountains
6. **How does the climate affect the way we make a living?**
   It affects how we use the lands

Think ahead: How does the climate affect jobs in the community where you live?

Answer Key

Name _____ skill: comprehension

Farming

Farming is one important way of making a living. Farming gives people the food they need. The climate helps farmers know what crops to plant. Crops like wheat, corn, vegetables, and fruits are grown on farms. The food they grow will usually be canned or frozen so it can be shipped to other places. This way, people can buy the food they need in grocery stores. Climate also tells farmers when to plant the crop. If crops are planted too early, frost (tiny ice crystals) might ruin the plants. If there is too little or too much rainfall the crops may be ruined. If a crop is planted too late, there may not be enough time for it to grow before winter comes. Farmers know the climate and watch the weather to grow the best crops they can.

1. The main idea of this story is:
   a. Farmers grow food.
   b. Wheat and vegetables are crops.
   (c.) Climate has a big affect on farming.
2. Why is farming important to us?
   it gives people the food they need.
3. How do people in other places get some of the crops?
   It is shipped to them
4. What does the word "frost" mean?
   (a.) ice crystals
   b. snow
   c. heavy rain
5. How does climate affect when a crop is planted?
   If it is too early there may be frost, too late and there may not be enough growing time
6. Why do farmers think about the climate before they plant crops?
   to know which crops to plant.

Think ahead: What crops are grown in your area?

©1995 Kelley Wingate Publications, Inc.   36   KW 1013

Name _____ skill: comprehension

Ranching

Ranching is another important way of making a living. A ranch is different from a farm. A farmer grows plants while a rancher raises, or grows, animals. Cattle, sheep, goats, and pigs are raised on ranches. These animals give us meat or other products we use every day. Some ranchers have milk cows. They are milked every day. The milk is made into cheese, cream, butter, and milk. Other ranchers raise cows for the meat and leather. These cows are butchered, or killed, to give us meat to eat. The hides, or skin, are used to make leather products like belts, purses, and shoes. Goat and sheep ranchers shear, or cut the hair and wool, from their animals. The hair is sold and made into yarn and cloth for us to wear. Some sheep and pigs, like some cows, are grown for their meat. All of these animals, and the ranches they live on, are important to our lives.

1. The main idea of this story is:
   a. Ranches grow animals.
   (b.) Ranches give us products we use every day.
   c. Sheep and cows are raised on ranches.
2. Why is ranching important to us?
   They give us things we use
3. What products do we get from cows?
   cheese, cream, butter, milk, meat
4. What does the word "shear" mean?
   a. kill
   b. skin
   (c.) cut
5. What is another word for "skin of an animal"?
   a. butcher
   (b.) hide
   c. to cut wool
6. What products do we get from sheep?
   wool and meat.

Think ahead: What products have you used today that came from a ranch?

©1995 Kelley Wingate Publications, Inc.   37   KW 1013

Name _____ skill: comprehension

Mining

In some parts of the world we can find minerals. Minerals are solid materials that are made by nature. Some minerals are oil, coal, and diamonds. Mining, or digging out, the minerals is one way to make a living. Oil is used in many ways. We use oil to make gasoline, ink, paints, plastics, and even lipstick! Oil is mined by deep wells that are dug into the earth. Other minerals, like coal and diamonds, are mined by digging large tunnels into the earth. Men go into the tunnels and remove the minerals so we can use them for many different things. Some minerals are ores, or metals, and are also mined. Iron, copper, silver, and gold are ores that are smelted, or melted, to make metal. If these minerals were not mined, we would not have many of the products we use every day!

1. The main idea of this story is:
   (a.) We mine minerals to make many products.
   b. Oil is a useful mineral.
   c. Minerals help us in many ways.
2. Why is mining important to us?
   We get many things we use daily
3. How is oil mined?
   by deep wells dug into the earth
4. What does the word "smelt" mean?
   a. metal
   (b.) melt ores into metal
   c. to dig tunnels
5. How are most minerals mined?
   by digging
6. Name some products that are made from oil.
   gasoline, ink, paints, plastics, lipstick

Think ahead: What products do you use that are made from minerals?

©1995 Kelley Wingate Publications, Inc.   38   KW 1013

Name _____ skill: comprehension

Lumbering

Many things are made of wood. Tables, doors, homes, and paper are all made of wood. The job of getting the wood to make products is called lumbering. Lumbering in North America was first started in the northern forests. New England, New York, and Michigan had huge forests that were cleared, or cut, to make lumber. As these forests were used up, lumbering was done in the Appalachian Mountains and in the southeastern area. Today a lot of our lumber comes from the forests in the northwestern states. People who make a living cutting trees are called lumberjacks. The logs they cut are floated down rivers or trucked to sawmills where they are cut into boards, planks, and beams.

1. The main idea of this story is:
   a. Lumberjacks cut trees.
   b. Many products are made of wood.
   (c.) Lumbering is how we get wood for products.
2. Why is lumbering important to us?
   Many things are made of wood
3. Where did most of the early lumbering take place?
   In the northern forests
4. What does the word "cleared" mean?
   (a.) cut away
   b. lumber
   c. wood
5. How might climate affect where people get lumber?
   It affects where trees grow
6. How do cut trees get to sawmills?
   They are floated down rivers or trucked.

Think ahead: Name six things in your classroom that are made from wood.

©1995 Kelley Wingate Publications, Inc.   39   KW 1013

Answer Key

Name _____ skill: comprehension

Manufacturing

Most people in the United States make a living by manufacturing. Manufacture means to make a product. Nearly everything we use has been manufactured in a factory. Food products are canned, boxed, or frozen in factories before they are shipped to grocery stores. Clothing, cars, and chemicals are made in factories. Computers, pencils, and carpets are manufactured. Some factories are very small and can be run by one family. Many factories are very large and make thousands of products every day.

1. **The main idea of this story is:**
   a. Most products we use have been manufactured.
   b. Factories manufacture goods.
   c. Food products are made in factories.
2. **Why is manufacturing important to us?**

   Nearly everything we use
   has been manufactured.
3. **Name five products that are manufactured?**

   Food, clothing, cars, chemicals,
   computers, pencils, carpets

4. **What word means "to make a product"?**
   a. manufacture
   b. factory
   c. products
5. **How do most of the people your country make a living?**

Think ahead: Name six things in your classroom that were manufactured.

Name _____ skill: comprehension

Services

Many people make a living by selling their **services** to others. A service is work done for other people. Teachers, doctors, librarians, and bus drivers are service people. Waitresses, babysitters, and cab drivers are also service people. Many service people work for the government. Mail carriers, police officers, and firefighters work for the government. The leader of a government has a service job, too! It would be difficult to get through a day without the services these people provide, or give us.

1. **The main idea of this story is:**
   a. A doctor has a government job.
   b. Services help us every day.
   c. Teachers have service jobs.
2. **Why are services important to us?**

   They work for us.
3. **What does the word "service" mean?**
   a. work for pay
   b. help others
   c. work done for others
4. **Name four service jobs that are not listed in this passage.**

   cook, accountant, attorney,
   mechanic, etc.
5. **What is a word that means "to supply or give"?**
   a. service
   b. government
   c. provide
6. **What are three government service jobs?**

   mail carrier, police officer,
   firefighter

Think ahead: Name three services your family has used this week?

Name _____ skill: comprehension

Transportation

When North America was first developed you could move across the country by taking a wagon pulled by horses or oxen. It took months to travel from Totonto to California. You may have taken a ship, but it had to go around the whole continent and took even longer than the wagons. In 1869 railroads finally connected the east coast to the west coast. It became easier to travel and ship goods from one place to another. Today, highways and fast cars, trucks, or buses make it easy to go almost anywhere in just a few days. Airplanes can make the trip in just a few hours. All of these ways of getting from one place to another are forms of transportation. We use transportation to make life easier as we go to work, ship goods from one area to another, or visit with distant family.

1. **The main idea of this story is:**
   a. Transportation makes life easier.
   b. It took a long time to cross the United States by wagon.
   c. Cars, trains, and airplanes are forms of transportation.
2. **Why were railroads easier to travel by than wagons or ships?**

   they were faster
3. **What two ways did early settlers get from one side of the United States to the other?**

   wagons and ships
4. **What does the word "transportation" mean?**
   a. ways to travel
   b. trucks
   c. trains and airplanes
5. **How did the railroad make travel easier?**

   they were faster

6. **Why do we need fast ways to get to far places?**

   to go to work, ship goods, or
   visit family

Think ahead: What forms of transportation have you used this week?

Name _____ skill: comprehension

Communication

How do we communicate, or share information, with each other? We can talk to our parents and tell them about our day. We can use the telephone to talk to people in other places. We can listen to the radio and hear about things that are happening anywhere in the country or world! Talking is only one way to communicate. Newspapers, books, and magazines are also types of communication. We can share information by reading about it in print. We can find out about the past, about how to make things, or about science by reading what other people wrote in books. The television is a kind of communication that is almost like being there. Reporters show us live pictures and tell us what is happening in our community, country, and world. We can see what is happening without having to be there. Communication is a way of sharing information so that we all can learn what is happening anywhere in the world.

1. **The main idea of this story is:**
   a. Television is the best form of communication.
   b. Books and newspapers are kinds of communication
   c. Communication lets us share information
2. **Why is communication important to us?**

   We can share information
3. **How can we learn what is happening in other parts of the world?**

   reading and television
4. **What does the word "communicate" mean?**
   a. speak
   b. share information
   c. watch television
5. **Name five kinds of communication.**

   newspapers, books, magazines,
   telephones, radio, television
6. **Why is it important to have communication with the rest of the world?**

   so we know what is happening
   there

Think ahead: How could you communicate with a child in another country

---

Answer Key

Name _____ skill: comprehension

Foods

Years ago people ate only the foods that were found nearby. Transportation was not very good so food could not be shipped long distances. Because of this, food was not the same everywhere in the country. People in the north did not have fresh fruit or vegetables during the winter months. People in Illinois did not get oranges or grapefruit because they could not grow them. Today trains, trucks, and airplanes carry fresh food to many areas. You can eat a Washington apple in Mississippi. You can have Florida oranges in Ontario. You can eat Maine lobster in Montreal. It is even possible to find food and spices from other countries in your local, or nearby, grocery store! Now everyone can have the food they need or want at any time of the year.

1. The main idea of this story is:
   a. Better transportation helps us get fresh food.
   b. Food could not be shipped far or it would spoil.
   c. Food is important to us.
2. How did people used to get food?

   They found it nearby

3. How do people get fresh food from other places?

   trains, trucks, and airplanes carry it

4. What word means "nearby"?
   a. possible
   b. transportation
   c. local
5. Why do we need to have foods from other places?

   So we can eat a balanced diet

6. Why might we want foods from other countries?

   for taste and variety

Think ahead: What foods from other countries can you find in your grocery store?

©1995 Kelley Wingate Publications, Inc.   44   KW 1013

Name _____ skill: comprehension

Homes

Are all homes the same? No, people live in many different kinds of homes. Some people have large homes with big yards. Others live in apartments with no yard at all. Houses do not all look the same. They are not all made from the same materials, or supplies, either. Some houses are made of wood. Others are made of brick or stone. The climate of an area affects how homes are designed, or planned. Homes in the northern areas are built with insulated, or padded, walls to keep the cold out. Most homes in the southern areas have air conditioning, or cooling systems, to protect them from the hot summers. Homes that are near rivers or swamps that flood in the spring are often built on stilts off the ground. When the water rises, the homes are kept safe above it all. Homes that are built to fit the climate are much more comfortable to live in!

1. The main idea of this story is:
   a. Homes are built differently.
   b. All homes are the same.
   c. Some homes are made of wood and others of brick.
2. Why are homes important to us?

   they are where we live

3. What does the word "design" mean in this passage?
   a. color
   b. plan
   c. draw
4. What is another word for "padded"?
   a. insulated
   b. comfortable
   c. cooled
5. Why do homes in the south need to be air conditioned?

   to protect us from the hot summers

6. Why don't we build all homes alike?

   because the climate is different in different areas

Think ahead: What special features does your home have that protects you from the climate?

©1995 Kelley Wingate Publications, Inc.   45   KW 1013

Name _____ skill: comprehension

Clothing

The clothes we wear are much the same all over the country. We all have shirts, pants, dresses, and socks. However, the climate we live in does cause us to wear certain things more often than we would if we lived somewhere else. It also helps us choose the materials we use to make the clothes. In cold climates people dress to keep warm. Wool from sheep is clipped and made into yarn for sweaters or cloth for warm clothes. In warm climates, people wear lighter clothing. Cotton is grown in warm parts of our country and we use it to make cool, comfortable shirts and slacks. Silk, another lightweight material, comes from the silkworm. We usually get silk from other countries like China or Japan. In wet climates most people have raincoats and boots handy to protect them from the rain. Many of the things we use to protect us from the rain are made from rubber or plastic. Rubber comes from trees in tropical, or very hot and wet, places. We use rubber for boots and shoe bottoms. Plastic is made in factories. Many umbrellas and raincoats are made from plastic. Plastic is also used to make nylon and rayon, materials that are used for many different kinds of clothes.

1. The main idea of this story is:
   a. Plastic is used in many materials.
   b. Wool is used in colder climates.
   c. Clothing helps protect us from the climate.
2. How does the climate affect what we wear?

   we dress to stay warm, cool or dry

3. Where does silk come from?

   Silkworms in China or Japan

4. What does the word "tropical" mean?
   a. a kind of plastic
   b. rainy
   c. hot and wet
5. Where does rubber come from?

   trees in tropical places

6. Why do we use different materials to make our clothes?

   because they can do different things for us.

Think ahead: What kind of clothes do you need for the climate you live in?

©1995 Kelley Wingate Publications, Inc.   46   KW 1013

Name _____ skill: comprehension

Harming the Earth

We have learned that we use many things from the earth. Minerals, trees, water, and plants are resources (things that take care of our needs) that we get from the earth. We use the resources to make life better for ourselves. We must also be careful not to ruin the earth by abusing, or misusing, these resources. A farmer must rotate, or change, crops every few years or he can ruin the soil. Lumberjacks must plant new trees to replace the ones they cut or we will run out of trees before long. Manufacturers cannot dump chemicals into rivers or bury them because they may poison our water and soil. The earth gives us so much. We must be careful not to waste our resources. We must conserve (take care of and protect) our natural resources so that they will be here for years to come.

1. The main idea of this story is:
   a. We must protect the earth by conserving our resources.
   b. The earth gives us natural resources.
   c. Manufacturers are ruining our water and land.
2. How are natural resources important to us?

   they make life better for us

3. What is another word for "misusing"?
   a. resources
   b. abusing
   c. conserving
4. What does the word "rotate" mean?
   a. change
   b. replant
   c. soil
5. Name two ways we can abuse our resources.

   dumping chemicals, cutting too many trees

6. Name two ways we can conserve resources.

   rotate crops, plant new trees, not waste water

Think ahead: What are some ways your community tries to conserve resources?

©1995 Kelley Wingate Publications, Inc.   47   KW 1013

Answer Key

Name _____ skill: comprehension

Ecology

The study of living things and how they depend on the world around them is called ecology. People depend on the earth to provide natural resources. We use the resources to live and to make our lives easier. Nature can keep itself balanced (even or steady) if left alone. People have to use the plants and animals for food and materials they need to survive. People also destroy many plants and animal carelessly. They cut down rain forests to use the trees, destroying plants and animals that help keep nature balanced. People throw trash in the oceans and poison our water and land with chemicals that are no longer useable. Nature is not able to get rid of the waste as fast as we dump it. We must be careful with the way we use the earth, or we may end up without the resources we need.

1. The main idea of this story is:
    a. Man depends on resources.
    b. The earth cannot get rid of our waste fast enough.
    c. Man must learn to use nature wisely. *(circled)*
2. What is ecology?

The study of living things and how they depend on the earth

3. How are people ruining the earth?

Carelessness, cutting forests, littering

4. What does the word "balanced" mean?
    a. resources
    b. even or steady *(circled)*
    c. survive
5. Can we stop using resources?

No, people need them to survive

6. What can we do to help nature stay balanced?

be careful with the way we use the earth

Think ahead: What may happen if man continues to waste natural resources?

Name _____ skill: context clues

Using Context Clues

When you come to a word you don't know, use the **context clues** (other words around it) to help you figure out the meaning.

Use context clues to figure out the meaning of each underlined word below. Circle the correct meaning.

1. The green light coming from the haunted house was frightening. It was an eerie sight!
    a. green   b. spooky *(circled)*   c. funny

2. The man bellows at his family when he gets very angry.
    a. laughs   b. eats   c. shouts *(circled)*

3. The clasp of the seat belt was not fastened correctly.
    a. buckle *(circled)*   b. strap   c. seat

4. We must leave soon. We will depart as soon as everyone is ready.
    a. watch   b. leave *(circled)*   c. sign

5. I have an errand to do for my mother. She wants me to go to the store for her.
    a. job *(circled)*   b. bag   c. test

6. When my sister found out I broke her toy she was furious with me.
    a. very pleased   b. very tired   c. very angry *(circled)*

7. Your must insert a nickel in the machine to get a gum ball.
    a. put in *(circled)*   b. take out   c. hand over

8. Jack is asleep in class. Nudge him with your elbow to wake him up.
    a. sweep   b. signal   c. push *(circled)*

Name _____ skill: context clues

Using Context Clues

When you come to a word you don't know, use the **context clues** (other words around it) to help you figure out the meaning.

Use context clues to figure out the meaning of each underlined word below. Circle the correct meaning.

1. We need another plank for the floor of our clubhouse. It should be about six feet long.
    a. nail   b. board *(circled)*   c. hammer

2. My new sweater is the most recent style. It was just designed last week.
    a. oldest   b. newest *(circled)*   c. youngest

3. I was so embarrassed, my face turned crimson.
    a. red *(circled)*   b. white   c. cold

4. I really blundered when I gave the wrong answer on the test.
    a. danced   b. laughed   c. made a mistake *(circled)*

5. The children clustered around their teacher when they went into the snake exhibit. Most of them were a little scared.
    a. jumped   b. slept   c. gathered *(circled)*

6. We are on the second floor. You must descend the stairs to get to the first floor.
    a. go down *(circled)*   b. go up   c. go around

7. The children were exhausted after running five miles.
    a. awake   b. tired *(circled)*   c. ready to run

8. Would you sketch a quick house for me. Use the white paper and a pencil.
    a. build   b. draw *(circled)*   c. play

Name _____ skill: context clues

Using Context Clues

When you come to a word you don't know, use the **context clues** (other words around it) to help you figure out the meaning.

Use context clues to figure out the meaning of each underlined word below. Circle the correct meaning.

1. His mouth was gaping when he yawned.
    a. wide open *(circled)*   b. closed   c. smiling

2. Katie was a loyal friend. She would not tell my secret even when they called her names.
    a. mean   b. playful   c. true *(circled)*

3. My arm was numb after I slept on it all night.
    a. unfeeling *(circled)*   b. thick   c. important

4. We used an old rag to plug the hole in the boat. That kept the water from coming in.
    a. to cut out   b. to stop up *(circled)*   c. to paint

5. I will release your hand if you promise not to write on me.
    a. let go of *(circled)*   b. twist   c. hold

6. Don't dawdle. We must be ready in just five minutes!
    a. waste time *(circled)*   b. hurry   c. get dressed

7. Tie your new bonnet under your chin. It will shade your head from the hot sun.
    a. umbrella   b. coat   c. hat *(circled)*

8. We must crate the dishes so they won't break in the moving van.
    a. box *(circled)*   b. make   c. drop

Answer Key

Name _____ skill: context clues

Using Context Clues

When you come to a word you don't know, use the **context clues** (other words around it) to help you figure out the meaning.

Use context clues to figure out the meaning of each underlined word below.
Circle the correct meaning.

1. I detest having my teeth pulled!
   a. enjoy   (b. hate)   c. fix

2. Take the lid off the box and expose what is inside so we can all see.
   (a. uncover)   b. break   c. send

3. Jason fell off his bike when he rode in the loose gravel. The sharp edges cut his knees.
   a. sand   (b. pebbles)   c. grass

4. It had not rained in a long time. It was so dry that the sod in my front yard was turning brown.
   a. sand   b. pebbles   (c. grass)

5. Observe the bird and see if you can find where she hid her nest.
   (a. study)   b. call to   c. feather

6. My sister took her time easing into the cold water. I plunged right in.
   a. waded   b. sat   (c. dived)

7. This job requires a hammer and nails.
   (a. needs)   b. looks at   c. sits down

8. The jagged edge of the broken window was dangerous.
   (a. pointed)   b. smooth   c. easy

©1995 Kelley Wingate Publications, Inc.   52   KW 1013

Name _____ skill: context clues

Using Context Clues

When you come to a word you don't know, use the **context clues** (other words around it) to help you figure out the meaning.

Use context clues to figure out the meaning of each underlined word below.
Circle the correct meaning.

1. Please keep your answer brief. A "yes" or "no" is enough.
   a. long   b. fancy   (c. short)

2. The boy was cruel to the dog. He beat it with a stick.
   (a. mean)   b. nice   c. kind

3. Frank wore fake glasses and a wig. He disguised himself.
   a. painted   (b. hid)   c. liked

4. Do not leave your swimsuit in the sun because the colors may fade.
   (a. lose color)   b. darken   c. wave

5. Bill was full of grief when his dog ran away. He cried himself to sleep.
   a. happiness   b. anger   (c. sadness)

6. Do not mingle your crayons with mine. I don't want to get any of yours by mistake.
   a. bend   (b. mix together)   c. use

7. A wonderful odor was coming from the kitchen while mother baked cookies.
   a. taste   b. sound   (c. smell)

8. Evie put her money in the pouch she wore on her belt.
   (a. bag)   b. paper   c. shirt

©1995 Kelley Wingate Publications, Inc.   53   KW 1013

Name _____ skill: context clues

Using Context Clues

When you come to a word you don't know, use the **context clues** (other words around it) to help you figure out the meaning.

Use context clues to figure out the meaning of each underlined word below.
Circle the correct meaning.

1. Joe did not respond when Alice asked him a question. He was asleep and did not hear her.
   (a. answer)   b. read   c. eat

2. The icy sidewalk was so slick, Ann fell down when she stepped on it.
   a. wet   b. pretty   (c. slippery)

3. Use the big shears to cut that paper.
   a. ruler   (b. scissors)   c. pencil

4. The fox had a cunning plan to catch the rabbit.
   (a. clever)   b. cloudy   c. fast

5. Six brown puppies were on display in the pet store window.
   (a. put out for show)   b. digging   c. furry

6. Mother told me I did a great job. She knows how to flatter me.
   a. holler at   (b. praise)   c. smile

7. A gust of wind took my kite higher than ever before!
   a. small   b. storm   (c. blast)

8. The small boy got into a lot of mischief at school. His mother had to come and get him.
   (a. trouble)   b. goodness   c. fun

©1995 Kelley Wingate Publications, Inc.   54   KW 1013

Name _____ skill: context clues

Using Context Clues

When you come to a word you don't know, use the **context clues** (other words around it) to help you figure out the meaning.

Use context clues to figure out the meaning of each underlined word below.
Circle the correct meaning.

1. I try to avoid things I don't like.
   a. get close to   (b. stay away from)   c. eat

2. We must use caution when crossing a busy street.
   a. feet   b. hurry   (c. be careful)

3. The kitten had dainty little feet. They were tinier than my thumb!
   (a. small)   b. furry   c. nice

4. I dodged when my brother threw the towel at my face.
   (a. ducked down)   b. smiled   c. got wet

5. The mother was frantic when her little girl was lost in the store.
   (a. wild with worry)   b. a little upset   c. laughing

6. It is not a good day to be outside. The snow and wind are harsh.
   a. bright and pretty   b. windy and mild   (c. cutting and sharp)

7. It rained last night. I can tell because the ground is still moist.
   a. dry   (b. wet)   c. warm

8. Andy had to go pick up his parcel at the post office. It was too large to fit in his mailbox.
   (a. package)   b. stamps   c. bills

©1995 Kelley Wingate Publications, Inc.   55   KW 1013

©1995 Kelley Wingate Publications, Inc.   115   CD-3710

Answer Key

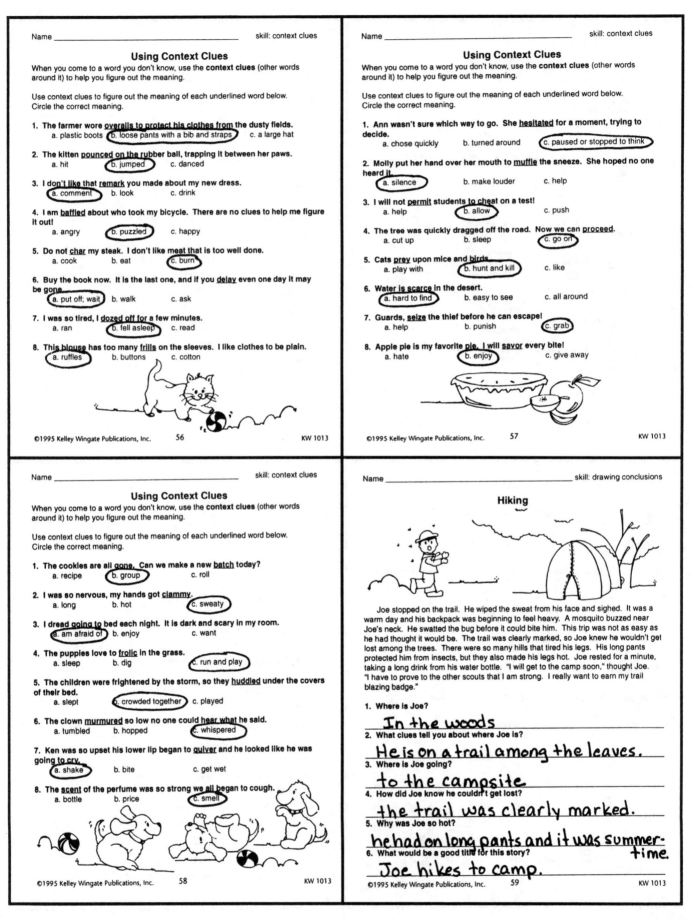

Name _____   skill: context clues

Using Context Clues

When you come to a word you don't know, use the **context clues** (other words around it) to help you figure out the meaning.

Use context clues to figure out the meaning of each underlined word below. Circle the correct meaning.

1. The farmer wore <u>overalls to protect his clothes from</u> the dusty fields.
   a. plastic boots   **b. loose pants with a bib and straps**   c. a large hat

2. The kitten <u>pounced on the rubber ball</u>, trapping it between her paws.
   a. hit   **b. jumped**   c. danced

3. I <u>don't like</u> that <u>remark</u> you made about my new dress.
   a. comment   b. look   c. drink

4. I am <u>baffled</u> about who took my bicycle. There are no clues to help me figure it out!
   a. angry   **b. puzzled**   c. happy

5. Do not <u>char</u> my steak. I don't like meat that is too well done.
   a. cook   b. eat   **c. burn**

6. Buy the book now. It is the last one, and if you <u>delay</u> even one day it may be gone.
   a. put off; wait   b. walk   c. ask

7. I was so tired, I <u>dozed off</u> for a few minutes.
   a. ran   **b. fell asleep**   c. read

8. This blouse has too many <u>frills</u> on the sleeves. I like clothes to be plain.
   a. ruffles   b. buttons   c. cotton

©1995 Kelley Wingate Publications, Inc.   56   KW 1013

Name _____   skill: context clues

Using Context Clues

When you come to a word you don't know, use the **context clues** (other words around it) to help you figure out the meaning.

Use context clues to figure out the meaning of each underlined word below. Circle the correct meaning.

1. Ann wasn't sure which way to go. She <u>hesitated</u> for a moment, trying to decide.
   a. chose quickly   b. turned around   **c. paused or stopped to think**

2. Molly put her hand over her mouth to <u>muffle</u> the sneeze. She hoped no one heard it.
   a. silence   b. make louder   c. help

3. I will not <u>permit</u> students to cheat on a test!
   a. help   **b. allow**   c. push

4. The tree was quickly dragged off the road. Now we can <u>proceed</u>.
   a. cut up   b. sleep   **c. go on**

5. Cats <u>prey</u> upon mice and birds.
   a. play with   **b. hunt and kill**   c. like

6. Water is <u>scarce</u> in the desert.
   a. hard to find   b. easy to see   c. all around

7. Guards, <u>seize</u> the thief before he can escape!
   a. help   b. punish   **c. grab**

8. Apple pie is my favorite pie. I will <u>savor</u> every bite!
   a. hate   **b. enjoy**   c. give away

©1995 Kelley Wingate Publications, Inc.   57   KW 1013

Name _____   skill: context clues

Using Context Clues

When you come to a word you don't know, use the **context clues** (other words around it) to help you figure out the meaning.

Use context clues to figure out the meaning of each underlined word below. Circle the correct meaning.

1. The cookies are all <u>gone</u>. Can we make a new <u>batch</u> today?
   a. recipe   **b. group**   c. roll

2. I was so nervous, my hands got <u>clammy</u>.
   a. long   b. hot   **c. sweaty**

3. I <u>dread going to</u> bed each night. It is dark and scary in my room.
   a. am afraid of   b. enjoy   c. want

4. The puppies love to <u>frolic</u> in the grass.
   a. sleep   b. dig   **c. run and play**

5. The children were frightened by the storm, so they <u>huddled</u> under the covers of their bed.
   a. slept   **b. crowded together**   c. played

6. The clown <u>murmured</u> so low no one could <u>hear what</u> he said.
   a. tumbled   b. hopped   **c. whispered**

7. Ken was so upset his lower lip began to <u>quiver</u> and he looked like he was going to cry.
   a. shake   b. bite   c. get wet

8. The <u>scent</u> of the perfume was so strong we all began to cough.
   a. bottle   b. price   **c. smell**

©1995 Kelley Wingate Publications, Inc.   58   KW 1013

Name _____   skill: drawing conclusions

Hiking

Joe stopped on the trail. He wiped the sweat from his face and sighed. It was a warm day and his backpack was beginning to feel heavy. A mosquito buzzed near Joe's neck. He swatted the bug before it could bite him. This trip was not as easy as he had thought it would be. The trail was clearly marked, so Joe knew he wouldn't get lost among the trees. There were so many hills that tired his legs. His long pants protected him from insects, but they also made his legs hot. Joe rested for a minute, taking a long drink from his water bottle. "I will get to the camp soon," thought Joe. "I have to prove to the other scouts that I am strong. I really want to earn my trail blazing badge."

1. Where is Joe?
   In the woods

2. What clues tell you about where Joe is?
   He is on a trail among the leaves.

3. Where is Joe going?
   to the campsite

4. How did Joe know he couldn't get lost?
   the trail was clearly marked.

5. Why was Joe so hot?
   he had on long pants and it was summertime.

6. What would be a good title for this story?
   Joe hikes to camp.

©1995 Kelley Wingate Publications, Inc.   59   KW 1013

©1995 Kelley Wingate Publications, Inc.   116   CD-3710

Answer Key

Name _____ skill: drawing conclusions

The Surprise

Karen got out scissors and tape. She took them to her bedroom. Then she went to the closet and quietly opened the door. She looked over the rolls of wrapping paper and chose the green one with yellow horns and party blowers printed on it. Karen quietly closed the door and tip-toed back to her room. She closed and locked the bedroom door. Safe at last! Karen pulled a paper bag from under her bed. She was careful not to rattle the paper too much. She didn't want her sister to hear what she was doing. Karen had saved her allowance for five weeks to buy the red sweater that was in the bag. It was such a beautiful sweater. Her sister had really liked it when they saw it for the first time in the store window. Karen carefully wrapped the sweater in the green paper. She signed the card and taped it to the package. What a good surprise this would be!

1. Where does most of this story take place?

In Karen's bedroom

2. Why was Karen being so quiet?

She wanted to surprise her sister

3. Who is the sweater for?

her sister

4. What clues tell you who the sweater is for?

Karen's sister liked the sweater in the store.

5. How long had Karen saved to buy the sweater?

five weeks

6. What do you think is the reason Karen is trying to surprise her sister?

It might be her birthday

©1995 Kelley Wingate Publications, Inc.   60   KW 1013

Name _____ skill: drawing conclusions

The Contest

Marcie's face was red and tears stung her eyes. She blinked and swallowed hard. She would not cry. Not now in front of all these people. She was angry with herself. What a silly mistake. She knew the right answer so why had she given the wrong one? The boy in the seat next to her leaned forward. The teacher asked him the same question she had just asked Marcie. The boy answered it correctly. The audience clapped and cheered for him. He had won. "It just isn't fair," thought Marcie. She really knew, though, that it was fair. She had been too nervous and had answered without thinking carefully. She turned to the boy and shook his hand. "You did a good job," she told him. She was glad it was over. She knew that next year she would do even better.

1. How did Marcie feel in the beginning of the story?

She felt embarrassed.

2. What clues tell you how she felt?

Her face was red. She swallowed hard.

3. What were Marcie, the boy, and the teacher doing?

a contest

4. Who won?

the boy

5. Was Marcie a good sport? Explain.

yes, she congratulated the boy.

6. What was Marcie planning at the end of the story?

to do better next year

©1995 Kelley Wingate Publications, Inc.   61   KW 1013

Name _____ skill: drawing conclusions

Picnic

Mother took out the bread, peanut butter, and jam. Brian and Kelsey made six sandwiches. They wrapped them in waxed paper. They put the sandwiches into the brown straw basket. Father filled a bottle with cold lemonade. "The sky is clear today," he smiled. "There won't be any rain to bother us!" Brian and Kelsey cut apples and carrots. They put the pieces into a plastic bag and added some grapes. Mother put a bag of cookies and some napkins into the basket. "The food is ready. Let's load the car," she said. Brian got the old blanket for sitting on the ground. He tossed it into the trunk. Kelsey gathered a few lawn games and some cards so they would have something to play. "We haven't done this in a long time," Kelsey laughed. "I hope the ants don't know we're coming!"

1. What is the family going to do?

Go on a picnic

2. What clues tell you about what they are going to do?

Packing food and a blanket

3. What are they taking to eat?

sandwiches, apples, grapes, carrots, cookies

4. Why did Brian bring the old blanket?

to cover the ground for sitting

5. Why was Father looking at the sky?

to see if it was going to rain.

6. What kind of sandwiches did they make?

peanut butter and jam

©1995 Kelley Wingate Publications, Inc.   62   KW 1013

Name _____ skill: drawing conclusions

Photograph

Jack was not comfortable. His new shirt was too stiff and his tie felt tight. Mother had fussed over his hair trying to get it to look just right. She made him scrub his hands three times to get all the dirt from under his fingernails! Finally his mom said he was ready. She smiled and said Jack looked very handsome in his suit. Jack frowned, but knew he could not tell his mom how he felt. This seemed to be very important to her. Jack sat on a special stool that turned and looked at the camera. He didn't feel like smiling at the lens, but he did his best. "Perfect!" smiled the man behind the camera as he snapped the shot. Jack posed two more times and then the man said they were finished. The first thing he did was take off his tie. Boy did that feel better!

1. What is Jack doing?

Having his picture taken

2. What clues tell you where Jack is?

sitting on stool, looking at camera

3. How does Jack feel about this?

he does not want to be doing it

4. What clues tell you how Jack feels?

his shirt was too stiff and his tie felt tight.

5. Who is the man that said "Perfect!"?

the photographer

6. Why did Jack take off his tie?

It was not comfortable

©1995 Kelley Wingate Publications, Inc.   63   KW 1013

Answer Key

Name _____ skill: drawing conclusions

Skiing

The hill looked really high from the top. The snow sparkled in the bright sun. It was pretty to look at, but Eric wasn't thinking about that. His stomach was fluttering and his hands began to sweat. He checked his boot straps. "See you at the bottom!" called Jessie. Eric watched as Jessie swished down the hill. Jessie was Eric's best friend, but at this moment Eric was not too happy with him. Jessie had talked Eric into trying this hill and now he was gone, leaving Eric by himself. Eric grasped the poles in his mittened hands. He hoped he would make it to the bottom without falling. This was the highest slope he had ever tried. "I can do this," he told himself firmly. Eric bent his knees and pushed off with the poles.

1. What is Eric doing?

skiing

2. Which clues tell you?

hilltop snow, boot straps, swished down the hill

3. How does Eric feel about this?

nervous

4. Why does he feel that way?

This was the highest slope she had ever tried.

5. Who is Jessie?

Eric's friend

6. Does Jessie feel the same way Eric does? Explain.

No, Jessie has already gone down the hill

©1995 Kelley Wingate Publications, Inc.   64   KW 1013

Name _____ skill: drawing conclusions

Blackie is Lost

Kevin sat on his front porch. His head rested on his hands and his mouth was turned down at the corners. Where could Blackie be? Kevin had called and looked all over the neighborhood but couldn't find his friend. Kevin looked at the bone Blackie had left on the bottom step. Blackie always had that bone in her mouth. It was her favorite toy. Kevin did not know what to do. Blackie had been gone for four hours and could be miles away by now. Kevin heard a faint whine come from under the porch. He got down on his hands and knees and peered into the darkness. There was Blackie lying near the house! Her tail began to thump but she did not get up. Kevin saw something wiggling near Blackie's stomach. Puppies! Blackie had hidden to have her babies. Kevin laughed and went to get Mother.

1. How did Kevin feel at the beginning of the story.

sad

2. Which clues tell you how Kevin felt?

mouth was turned down at the corners

3. Who is Blackie?

Kevin's dog

4. What did Kevin think had happened to Blackie?

He thought she was lost

5. What had really happened to Blackie?

She hid under the house to have puppies.

6. How do you think Kevin felt at the end of the story?

happy

©1995 Kelley Wingate Publications, Inc.   65   KW 1013

Name _____ skill: drawing conclusions

A Visit to the City

TRAIN STATION

Harry looked at his watch again. Time seems to go slowly when you are waiting. He picked up a newspaper and tried to read. The bustle of the station was too loud. He could not read here. Harry gave up trying and tossed the paper on the empty seat next to him. He hoped Kim would like the city. Harry had enjoyed visiting Kim's farm last summer. Now she was coming to see his city. Harry heard the whistle and the click-clack as the wheels rolled along the track. Kim was here! Harry waited as the passengers stepped down from the cars. Finally he saw Kim step down. "Welcome to Kingston!" he greeted her.

1. Where was Harry waiting?

In the train station

2. Which clues tell you where he is?

The bustle of the station was loud.

3. How did Harry feel as he waited?

nervous

4. Which clues helped you figure out how he felt?

he kept looking at his watch and couldn't read

5. Had Kim been to Kingston before?

no

6. Where had Harry been last summer?

visiting Kim's farm

©1995 Kelley Wingate Publications, Inc.   66   KW 1013

Name _____ skill: drawing conclusions

The Computer

John turned on the hard drive and watched the screen light up. He gathered his papers and began to type. The keyboard clacked as his fingers moved quickly over it. He had to get the letter printed before closing time. His boss had said the letter must be mailed today. John looked at the large clock over his desk. Would he finish in time? Soon the letter was typed. He ran the spelling program to see if there were any spelling errors. There were no mistakes! Just two minutes until closing time. John pressed the print button and watched as the letter magically appeared on the paper. He folded the letter, put it in an envelope, and put a stamp on the corner. He made it just in time!

1. What was John doing?

Typing a letter

2. Where is John?

In an office

3. Which clues helped you decide where John is?

His boss told him to hurry.

4. What kind of machine is John using?

a computer

5. What clues help tell you about the machine?

It has a keyboard and printer

6. How do you think John felt as she stamped the letter?

happy

©1995 Kelley Wingate Publications, Inc.   67   KW 1013

Answer Key

Name _____ skill: drawing conclusions

Baking a Cake

Betty put the flour, eggs, sugar, and milk on the table. She got out her biggest bowl and mixing spoons. Her recipe was old, but she knew how great it tasted. Betty carefully measured the flour and sugar. She broke the eggs and added the milk. She stirred carefully and read the recipe often to be sure she was doing everything the right way. Betty mixed the batter until is was smooth. She poured it into a pan and popped it into the oven. Soon the warm smell of her baking filled the house. Oh, did it smell good! At the right time, Betty took the pan from the oven and set it near the window to cool. She would frost it and take it to the bake sale first thing tomorrow morning.

1. What was Betty doing?
   baking
2. Which clues help you figure out what she is doing?
   bowl, mixing spoons, recipe, pans
3. What do you think Betty has made?
   a cake
4. Which clues help you figure out what Betty has made?
   she put the batter in the oven
5. What will Betty do with what she has made?
   take it to the bake sale
6. When will she finish?
   tomorrow

©1995 Kelley Wingate Publications, Inc.   68   KW 1013

Name _____ skill: predicting

Predicting

A.   Janice and Bill were going hiking. They had their lunches and water all packed and ready to go. Bill looked at the sky. The dark clouds were gathering and the wind was beginning to blow pretty hard.

1. What do you think Janice and Bill will do?
   not go hiking
2. Which clues helped you to decide?
   the clouds were dark, wind was blowing

B.   Joey was busy playing basketball with his friends. His shoelace was untied but he didn't want to stop to tie it. Each time he ran, the lace bounced against the ground. Joey almost stepped on it six different times. Kyle passed the ball to Joey. Here was his big chance to score and win the game! Joey began to dribble toward the basket.

1. What do you think will happen?
   he will trip on his shoelaces
2. Which clues helped you to decide?
   he stepped on it six times

C.   Mary awoke suddenly. Her room was very dark. She thought she heard a soft scratching sound at her window. There it was again! Mary's heart beat wildly. It might just be the tree branch rubbing her window. It could also be something else. Mary had to find out. She reached for the light switch on the lamp by her bed.

1. What do you think Mary did?
   turned on the light
2. Which clues helped you to decide?
   she was reaching for the switch

©1995 Kelley Wingate Publications, Inc.   69   KW 1013

Name _____ skill: predicting

Predicting

A.   Martin was riding his bike. He looked back to see if his friend was still behind him. Suddenly he heard the crunching of broken glass. Martin had ridden through the broken pieces of a bottle. His front tire began to wobble.

1. What do you think will happen?
   Martin's bike will get a flat tire
2. Which clues helped you to decide?
   He rode through glass, tire began to wobble

B.   Sally sneezed again. She couldn't believe it. Today was the one day she could go to the circus and she was not feeling very well. Her face was hot and her throat was sore. "Did I hear you sneeze?" asked her mother. Sally had never lied to her mother, but she knew she could not go to the circus if Mom knew she was sick.

1. What do you think Sally will tell her mother?
   that she did not sneeze
2. Which clues helped you to decide?
   she wanted to go to the circus

C.   The children were playing baseball in the empty lot. Peggy was up to bat. She swung hard and hit the ball further than anyone else had. The ball sailed across the lot and smashed through Mrs. Allen's window. Mrs. Allen was always yelling at the children to go somewhere else to play. Peggy knew she would really be angry this time. The other kids scattered, running for home. Peggy stood in the field looking at the broken window.

1. What do you think Peggy will do?
   Tell Mrs. Allen she broke the window
2. Which clues helped you to decide?
   Peggy stood looking at the broken window

©1995 Kelley Wingate Publications, Inc.   70   KW 1013

Name _____ skill: predicting

Predicting

A.   Buddy was excited. His parents had said he could stay up as late as he wanted tonight. He had begged them for weeks to stay up and watch television. Now he could watch all those late night movies! Buddy was sure he could stay up until dawn. Shortly after ten o'clock Buddy began to yawn. "I am not tired!" Buddy told himself. By 10:30 his eyes began to grow heavy. Buddy shook himself to wake up.

1. What do you think will happen to Buddy?
   He will fall asleep
2. Which clues helped you to decide?
   his eyes began to grow heavy, he shook himself

B.   The spaceship landed on the planet Vexia. This planet was a "dead" planet with no life on it. The captain decided to go outside the ship and look around. As he stepped out the door, the captain saw something strange.

1. What do you think the captain saw?
   Any answer of something unusual
2. Which clues helped you to decide?
   "dead planet", The captain saw something strange

C.   Andy had been told not to use his father's new telescope. But when he saw the puff of smoke over the woods behind the house, Andy knew he had to disobey. It had been a dry summer, and even a small fire in the woods would mean big trouble. Andy took the telescope to his treehouse and looked through it.

1. What do you think Andy saw?
   a fire
2. Which clues helped you to decide?
   a puff of smoke was over the woods

©1995 Kelley Wingate Publications, Inc.   71   KW 1013

Answer Key

Predicting

A. John was in a hurry. He had a new kite and he wanted to try it out before dinner. It was a box kite. John had never put together a box kite before. "Dinner in ten minutes," called his mother. John tossed the directions into the trash. He did not have time to read them now. John quickly put the pieces together. There were two sticks left over so he jammed them into his pocket. He ran to the field to try out the new kite.

1. What do you think will happen with John's kite?

The kite will not fly

2. Which clues helped you to decide?

had never made one before, threw away directions

B. Greg wanted to play ball but not one of his friends were at the playground. The only boy around was Jerry, a new kid in school. Jerry was quiet and had not seemed too friendly during school. Greg was about to go home when he noticed that Jerry was holding a baseball mitt. Greg thought for a few minutes then walked over to Jerry.

1. What do you think Greg will do?

ask the boy to play

2. Which clues helped you to decide?

Jerry wanted to play and Greg had a mitt

C. Kristin was trying out for the lead in the school play. She wanted to learn the lines and do well at try outs. Her friends, Sandy and Joan, wanted the same part. Every afternoon Sandy and Joan played at the park. They asked Kristin to play with them, but she went home and practiced her lines. On the day of try outs, the three girls took turns saying the lines.

1. Who do you think got the part?

Kristin got the part

2. Which clues helped you to decide?

she studied and practiced every day

©1995 Kelley Wingate Publications, Inc.   72   KW 1013

Predicting

A. Kelly wasn't sure what she should do. She needed ten more dollars to buy the bike helmet she wanted. Now her friend Patty wanted to buy her old roller skates for twelve dollars. Kelly had gotten new skates for her birthday and she really didn't need the old ones. But her parents had told her she must check with them before she could sell or give away any of her things.

1. What do you think Kelly will do?

Ask her parents first

2. Which clues helped you to decide?

her parents said she need to check with them first

B. The cold wind was blowing across town. Dark clouds gathered in the sky. The last few fall leaves danced on the wind as they let go of the bare tree limbs. Children hurried home to warm themselves. Their breath hung in little puffs in the air. The clouds grew darker and moved over the town.

1. What do you think will happen?

It will snow

2. Which clues helped you to decide?

cold wind, dark clouds, puffs of breath

C. Martha said she would help her neighbors while they were away. The neighbors said their plants needed a lot of water because they were about to bloom. Martha promised to water the garden every day while they were gone. The first day Martha watered all the plants. On the second day she forgot. It was such a warm day she stayed inside where it was cool. As a matter of fact, Martha forgot every day for a week.

1. What do you think happened to the garden?

it wilted or suffered in some way

2. Which clues helped you to decide?

Martha did not water the garden

©1995 Kelley Wingate Publications, Inc.   73   KW 1013

Compound words are two words put together to make a new word. For example, snow and man can be put together to make the new word "snowman". Make sense out of the story below by putting the compound words in the blanks where they belong.

backyard	campfire	fireflies	flashlight	lonesome
midnight	moonlight	rattlesnake	waterproof	weekend

Camping

Last _weekend_ I went camping. I had a _waterproof_ tent in case it rained. It was great fun at first. The _fireflies_ were glowing in the bushes. I built a warm _campfire_. The _moonlight_ was so bright I didn't even need my _flashlight_! About _midnight_ I became _lonesome_ and a little scared. I thought I heard a _rattlesnake_ near my tent. Thank goodness I was in my own _backyard_!

daylight	footprints	highway	lighthouse	rowboat
seashore	seaweed	sunlight	watermelon	grandmother

At The Beach

Ryan awoke when it was almost _daylight_. He got dressed and called to his _grandmother_. They got into the car and were soon on the _highway_ to the beach. When they saw the tall _lighthouse_ they knew they were almost to the _seashore_. Ryan ran across the sand, leaving _footprints_ as he ran. He played in the bright _sunlight_ all day. He gathered _seaweed_ and floated in a _rowboat_. For lunch they had a cold _watermelon_ to cool them off.

©1995 Kelley Wingate Publications, Inc.   74   KW 1013

Compound words are two words put together to make a new word. For example, snow and man can be put together to make the new word "snowman". Make sense out of the story below by putting the compound words in the blanks where they belong.

blackboard	breakfast	classroom	goodbye	homework
lunchroom	playground	schoolhouse	upstairs	windowsill

School

Caitlin likes to go to school. She eats _breakfast_, says _goodbye_, and walks to school. The _schoolhouse_ is two blocks from her house. Caitlin's _classroom_ is _upstairs_ on the second floor. Her teacher writes the date on the _blackboard_ each day. Her desk is near the window. If Caitlin leans on the _windowsill_ she can see the _playground_ with the swings below. At noon the class goes to the _lunchroom_ to eat. Caitlin enjoys the _homework_ she has to do every night!

backyard	bathroom	bedroom	birdhouse	clubhouse
countryside	doorstep	fireplace	mailbox	neighborhood

At Home

I like my house. We live in the _countryside_. Our _mailbox_ is in front of the house. There is a _birdhouse_ in the big maple tree. I have a _clubhouse_ in the _backyard_. My house has a large _fireplace_ where dad builds fires in the winter. My _bedroom_ is really nice. I even have my own _bathroom_ with a shower! I like to sit out front on the _doorstep_ because I can see the whole _neighborhood_ from there.

©1995 Kelley Wingate Publications, Inc.   75   KW 1013

Answer Key

Name _____ skill: compound words

Compound words are two words put together to make a new word. For example, snow and man can be put together to make the new word "snowman". Make sense out of the story below by putting the compound words in the blanks where they belong.

baseball	basketball	driveway	dugout	football
inside	outdoors	quarterback	racetrack	touchdowns

Sports Crazy

Last week Evan went sports crazy! Monday he played flag **football**. He was the **quarterback** and he made three **touchdowns**. Tuesday he went to the park to play **baseball**. He hit a fly ball and got a home run! His team in the **dugout** went wild. Wednesday Evan made a **racetrack** for his cars. Thursday it was too cold to play **outdoors** so Evan played **inside**. On Friday he shot baskets for three hours in his **driveway**. He said **basketball** is his favorite sport of all.

airplane	airport	afternoon	everywhere	headline
holdup	newspaper	policemen	Somebody	something

A Hero

Tyler was taking a trip. He went to the **airport** but **something** was wrong. Police cars were **everywhere**. Three **policemen** stood by the front door. **Somebody** said there was a famous thief on the **airplane**. A man jumped from the plane and began to run straight toward Tyler. Tyler stuck out his foot and tripped the man. Tyler was a hero! That **afternoon** Tyler's picture was in the **newspaper**. The **headline** said, "Tyler stops a **holdup**".

©1995 Kelley Wingate Publications, Inc.   76   KW 1013

Name _____ skill: compound words

Compound words are two words put together to make a new word. For example, snow and man can be put together to make the new word "snowman". Make sense out of the story below by putting the compound words in the blanks where they belong.

cowboy	firefighter	fisherman	grownup	mailman
policeman	railroad	somebody	storyteller	typewriter

What Will I Be?

When I am a **grownup** I want to have a good job. I will be a **policeman** and catch bad guys. I could also be a **firefighter** and drive a big red truck. I like to work on the **typewriter** so I could write books. I also like trains. I could work on the **railroad**. Dad says I am a great **fisherman** because I always catch the biggest fish. But I like horses, so I might just be a **cowboy**. Maybe I could be a **mailman** and deliver letters to far off places! Mom says that **somebody** with my imagination would make a good **storyteller**. What do you think I should be?

backpack	blackberries	blueberries	butterflies	daydream
footpath	lunchtime	nearby	strawberries	waterfall

A Walk In The Woods

Mary likes to take walks in the woods. She fills her **backpack** with food to eat at **lunchtime**. Along the path Mary finds **blackberries**, **blueberries**, and **strawberries** to pick. She knows a small stream that has a **waterfall**. She likes to sit near the splashing water and **daydream** about her life. There are a lot of pretty **butterflies** that flit on the **nearby** flowers. She follows the **footpath** home. What a wonderful way to spend a day!

©1995 Kelley Wingate Publications, Inc.   77   KW 1013

Name _____ skill: compound words

Compound words are two words put together to make a new word. For example, snow and man can be put together to make the new word "snowman". Make sense out of the story below by putting the compound words in the blanks where they belong.

candlelight	dinnertime	earthquake	fireworks	housetop
midnight	rainstorm	thunderbolt	Workmen	

The Storm

Last night, just before our **dinnertime**, we had a terrible storm. The thunder was so loud it shook the house like a little **earthquake**. The power went off and we had to eat dinner by **candlelight**. The **rainstorm** would not quit. A large **thunderbolt** struck our tree, knocking a branch into our **housetop**. The lightening was brighter than **fireworks** in July! By **midnight** the rain began to stop. The next morning the yard was a mess. **Workmen** had to clean up the broken tree branches. What a storm!

lonesome	anyone	homesick	rowboat	pancakes
breakfast	campfire	backward	anyone	into

Away At Camp

Last summer I went away to camp for a week. At first I felt **lonesome** because I didn't know **anyone**. The first night I was really **homesick**. The next day things got better. We made **pancakes** to eat for **breakfast**. We cooked them over the **campfire**. Later we took a **rowboat** across the lake. A boy named Jack stood up in the boat. He fell over **backward** and went into the lake before **anyone** could grab him. Jack wasn't hurt. He was just wet. I helped Jack get back **into** the boat. We became pals and I liked camp after that.

©1995 Kelley Wingate Publications, Inc.   78   KW 1013

Name _____ skill: word families: est, et

Word Families

Fill in the blank with the word that makes sense in the sentence.

best   nest   pest   rest   test   west

1. Cowboys live out **west**.

2. A bug can be a **pest**.

3. Baby birds live in a **nest**.

4. I am tired so I will **rest** now.

5. I think my drawing is the **best** one.

6. Today we had a **test** in math.

bet   get   let   net   Set   wet

1. I can **get** my own drink.

2. **Set** the book down right here.

3. We used a **net** to catch the fish.

4. Joe got **wet** in the rainstorm.

5. Please **let** me go to the show with you.

6. I **bet** you cannot do that!

©1995 Kelley Wingate Publications, Inc.   79   KW 1013

Answer Key

Word Families

Fill in the blank with the word that makes sense in the sentence.

| bow | crow | know | show | slow | throw |

1. A snail is a **slow** animal.
2. I **know** the answer!
3. Betsy has a **bow** in her hair.
4. John will **throw** the ball to me.
5. Listen to that rooster **crow** so early in the morning.
6. **Show** me where you got hurt.

| alive | arrive | chive | dive | five | hive |

1. **Five** pennies are the same amount as a nickel.
2. I will **arrive** at four o'clock.
3. Chris can **dive** into the pool.
4. A tree is **alive** but a rock is not.
5. Bees live in a **hive**.
6. A **chive** is a kind of onion.

Word Families

Fill in the blank with the word that makes sense in the sentence.

| day | lay | May | play | say | way |

1. This street goes only one **way**.
2. What did you **say**?
3. I will **lay** down and rest after my bath.
4. This has been a great **day**.
5. Will you **play** marbles with me?
6. **May** I have another cookie, please?

| chip | clip | sip | slip | tip | whip |

1. The **tip** of my pencil is broken.
2. A lion tamer uses a **whip**.
3. Do not **slip** on that wet floor.
4. There is a **chip** on the side of this glass.
5. May I have a **sip** of water?
6. Mother will **clip** the coupons from the paper.

Word Families

Fill in the blank with the word that makes sense in the sentence.

| brain | chain | drain | pain | rain | stain |

1. It looks like it might **rain** today.
2. The dog is on a long **chain**.
3. I have a **pain** in my back.
4. The grape juice will **stain** my shirt.
5. Let the water go down the **drain**.
6. My **brain** is not working well today!

| check | deck | fleck | neck | peck | wreck |

1. Wash the back of your **neck** well.
2. Mom wrote a **check** to pay for the groceries.
3. I play with a **deck** of cards.
4. There was a train **wreck** at the crossing last night.
5. The bird will **peck** at the seeds.
6. I see a **fleck** of paint on the floor.

Word Families

Fill in the blank with the word that makes sense in the sentence.

| age | cage | page | rage | stage | wage |

1. Turn to **page** five in your history book.
2. The play will be on the big **stage** in the auditorium.
3. My rabbit lives in a wire **cage**.
4. The man flew into an angry **rage** when we got away.
5. I am paid a **wage** for the work I do.
6. This fossil is from the **age** of dinosaurs.

| bump | dump | hump | jump | lump | stump |

1. I have a **lump** where the ball hit my head!
2. I did not mean to **bump** into you.
3. Can you **jump** rope with me today?
4. Please **dump** the trash in the can.
5. Some whales have a **hump** on their backs.
6. When they cut the tree down, only a **stump** was left.

Answer Key

Name _____ skill: word families: eam, ight

Word Families

Fill in the blank with the word that makes sense in the sentence.

cream   dream   gleam   seam   stream   team

1. The water is cold in that **stream**.
2. I tore the **seam** of my pants on the chair.
3. The child had a **gleam** in his eye when he understood.
4. At night I often **dream** of nice things.
5. Please put **cream** in my coffee.
6. I am on the baseball **team**.

delight   flight   light   might   night   right

1. I need a **light** because it is dark in my room.
2. Owls stay awake all **night**.
3. It is a **delight** to get a surprise!
4. Jason had his first **flight** on an airplane.
5. I **might** go to the zoo tomorrow.
6. This answer is the **right** one.

©1995 Kelley Wingate Publications, Inc.   84   KW 1013

Name _____ skill: word families: ake,ind

Word Families

Fill in the blank with the word that makes sense in the sentence.

brake   fake   lake   make   rake   stake

1. The diamond is a **fake**!
2. I must **brake** the car to a stop.
3. Hammer this tent **stake** into the ground.
4. In fall, we **rake** the leaves.
5. Can you **make** a snowman?
6. I would like to go swimming in the **lake**.

behind   blind   find   kind   rind   wind

1. I must **find** my lost mitten.
2. Everyday we **wind** the clock.
3. Put the lemon **rind** in the trash.
4. I was **blind** in the bright light.
5. I must hurry because I am **behind**.
6. Be **kind** to your friends.

©1995 Kelley Wingate Publications, Inc.   85   KW 1013

Name _____ skill: word families: ash,op

Word Families

Fill in the blank with the word that makes sense in the sentence.

ash   cash   lash   mash   rash   trash

1. Please **mash** the potatoes.
2. I have a red **rash** on my arms and face.
3. The fire left **ash** everywhere!
4. I need **cash** to buy this toy.
5. Put the **trash** in the litter can.
6. My **lash** fell on my cheek.

chop   crop   drop   mop   shop   stop

1. Do not **drop** that glass because it will break.
2. I can **mop** the floor tomorrow morning.
3. There is a **stop** sign at the next corner.
4. We **shop** in this store.
5. Corn is a good **crop** to grow.
6. My dad will **chop** the wood.

©1995 Kelley Wingate Publications, Inc.   86   KW 1013

Name _____ skill: word families: ace, are

Word Families

Fill in the blank with the word that makes sense in the sentence.

brace   face   grace   lace   pace   trace

1. There is **lace** on my new dress.
2. I need a **brace** for my broken arm.
3. Can you **trace** the picture for me?
4. The horse has a fast **pace**.
5. We say **grace** before we eat our dinner.
6. The clown has a painted **face**.

bare   care   flare   glare   mare   share

1. I do not **care** for a drink now.
2. Mother can really **flare** when she is angry.
3. The fire began to **glare** hotly.
4. I have **bare** legs when I wear shorts.
5. Will you **share** your lunch with me because I forgot mine?
6. That horse is a **mare**.

©1995 Kelley Wingate Publications, Inc.   87   KW 1013

Answer Key

Name _____ skill: word families: amp, ack

Word Families

Fill in the blank with the word that makes sense in the sentence.

camp   champ   Clamp   lamp   ramp   stamp

1. Put a **stamp** on the letter before you mail it.
2. **Clamp** the two pieces of wood together so I can glue them.
3. He won so he is the new **champ**
4. I like to **camp** in the woods.
5. I built a **ramp** for my skateboard jump.
6. This **lamp** gives off a lot of light.

back   rack   sack   snack   tack   track

1. The books are on a **rack** by the front door of the library.
2. My **back** hurts from lifting too much at once.
3. After school, Kelly has a **snack** because she is hungry.
4. I need a **tack** to keep this poster on the bulletin board.
5. My race cars go on a **track** .
6. I put the groceries in a paper **sack** .

©1995 Kelley Wingate Publications, Inc.   88   KW 10'

Name _____ skill: classification

Here is a list of words. They all have something in common. What heading can you give this list that will name all the words? Write the heading on the line "Main Heading". Divide the list into two groups that are alike. Put the title of each group on the lines "Subheading" and fill in the box with the correct subheading words.

apple   banana   beans   blueberry   broccoli   carrot   celery   cherry
cucumber   grape   lemon   lettuce   lime   onion   orange   pea   peach
pear   plum   pumpkin   potato   raspberry   spinach   squash

Main Heading Foods

Subheading: Fruit	Subheading: Vegetable
apple	beans
banana	broccoli
blueberry	carrot
grape	celery
orange	cucumber
peach	lettuce
pear	onion
plum	pea
raspberry	pumpkin
cherry	potato
lemon	spinach
lime	squash

©1995 Kelley Wingate Publications, Inc.   89   KW 1013

Name _____ skill: classification

Here is a list of words. They all have something in common. What heading can you give this list that will name all the words? Write the heading on the line "Main Heading". Divide the list into two groups that are alike. Put the title of each group on the lines "Subheading" and fill in the box with the correct subheading words.

alone   awful   blue   cheerful   down   funny   gay   glad   glum
good   hurt   jolly   joyful   low   moody   pleased   proud   sad
smiling   tearful   terrific   unhappy   unloved   wonderful

Main Heading Feelings

Subheading: Happy	Subheading: Sad
cheerful	alone
funny	awful
gay	blue
glad	down
good	glum
jolly	hurt
joyful	low
pleased	moody
proud	sad
smiling	tearful
terrific	unhappy
wonderful	unloved

©1995 Kelley Wingate Publications, Inc.   90   KW 1013

Name _____ skill: classification

Here is a list of words. They all have something in common. What heading can you give this list that will name all the words? Write the heading on the line "Main Heading". Divide the list into two groups that are alike. Put the title of each group on the lines "Subheading" and fill in the box with the correct subheading words.

big   bitty   enormous   fat   giant   gigantic   great   huge
large   little   long   mammoth   miniature   petite   short   skinny
slight   small   tall   teeny   thin   tiny   vast   wee

Main Heading Size

Subheading: big	Subheading: small
big	bitty
enormous	little
fat	miniature
giant	petite
gigantic	short
great	skinny
huge	slight
large	small
long	teeny
mammoth	thin
tall	tiny
vast	wee

©1995 Kelley Wingate Publications, Inc.   91   KW 1013

Answer Key

Name _____   skill: classification

Here is a list of words. They all have something in common. What heading can you give this list that will name all the words? Write the heading on the line "Main Heading". Divide the list into two groups that are alike. Put the title of each group on the lines "Subheading" and fill in the box with the correct subheading words.

draw   drew   hid   hide   jump   jumped   knew   know   sat
sit   stand   stood   swam   swim   tell   threw   throw   told
wake   win   woke   won   write   wrote

Main Heading __Verbs__

Subheading: past	Subheading: present
drew	draw
hid	hide
jumped	jump
knew	know
sat	sit
stood	stand
swam	swim
told	tell
threw	throw
woke	wake
won	win
wrote	write

Name _____   skill: classification

Here is a list of words. They all have something in common. What heading can you give this list that will name all the words? Write the heading on the line "Main Heading". Divide the list into three groups that are alike. Put the title of each group on the lines "Subheading" and fill in the box with the correct subheading words.

blizzard   bright   cloudless   cloudy   flurries   freeze   frozen
heat   hot   icy   pouring   puddles   sizzling   sleet
snow   snowflake   sprinkle   storm   sun   sunny
thunder   umbrella   warm   wet

Main Heading __Weather__

Subheading: Hot	Subheading: Cold	Subheading: Rainy
bright	blizzard	cloudy
cloudless	flurries	pouring
heat	freeze	puddles
hot	frozen	sprinkle
sizzling	icy	storm
sun	sleet	thunder
sunny	snow	umbrella
warm	snowflake	wet

Name _____   skill: classification

Here is a list of words. They all have something in common. What heading can you give this list that will name all the words? Write the heading on the line "Main Heading". Divide the list into three groups that are alike. Put the title of each group on the lines "Subheading" and fill in the box with the correct subheading words.

airplane   balloon   blimp   bus   canoe   car   jet
motorcycle   raft   rocket   rowboat   ship   space shuttle
submarine   train   truck   tugboat   van

Main Heading __transportation__

Subheading: land	Subheading: sea	Subheading: air
bus	canoe	airplane
motorcycle	raft	balloon
train	rowboat	blimp
truck	ship	jet
van	submarine	rocket
	tugboat	space shuttle

Name _____   skill: classification

Here is a list of words. They all have something in common. What heading can you give this list that will name all the words? Write the heading on the line "Main Heading". Divide the list into three groups that are alike. Put the title of each group on the lines "Subheading" and fill in the box with the correct subheading words.

auditorium   cafeteria   cafeteria server   classroom   crayons
English   eraser   Gym   History   janitor   librarian   library   Math
nurse   office   pen   pencil   playground   principal   ruler
Science   scissors   Social Studies   teacher

Main Heading __School things__

Subheading: Supplies	Subheading: Places	Subheading: Subjects	Subheading: People
crayons	auditorium	English	caf. server
eraser	cafeteria	History	janitor
pen	classroom	Math	librarian
pencil	Gym	Science	nurse
ruler	library	Soc. Studies	principal
scissors	office		teacher
	playground		

Answer Key

Name _____ skill: homonyms

Homonyms are words that sound the same but are spelled differently and do not mean the same thing. Choose the correct homonym for each blank.

ant   ate   aunt   eight   eye   I

1. My mother's sister is my **aunt**.
2. There is an **ant** hill in my front yard.
3. We **ate** dinner last night.
4. I have **eight** crayons in my box.
5. **I** want to play with you.
6. I have something in my **eye** and it really hurts!

ad   add   be   bee   berry   bury

1. We put an **ad** in the newspaper.
2. In math we **add** numbers together.
3. We will **be** leaving soon.
4. The **bee** makes honey in its hive.
5. Pick that big **berry** from the bush.
6. The dog will **bury** a bone.

©1995 Kelley Wingate Publications, Inc.   96   KW 1013

Name _____ skill: homonyms

Homonyms are words that sound the same but are spelled differently and do not mean the same thing. Choose the correct homonym for each blank.

blew   blue   brake   break   buy   by

1. The wind **blew** last night.
2. I have **blue** eyes.
3. The car **brake** did not stop us in time.
4. The glass will **break** if you drop it.
5. May we **buy** a new toy?
6. We walked **by** the library on our way home.

cent   scent   chews   choose   close   clothes

1. I have only one **cent** in my bank.
2. The skunk has a strong **scent** and it stinks.
3. The puppy **chews** on my shoes.
4. Please **choose** the one you like best.
5. You did not **close** the door tightly.
6. I wear warm **clothes** in winter.

©1995 Kelley Wingate Publications, Inc.   97   KW 1013

Name _____ skill: homonyms

Homonyms are words that sound the same but are spelled differently and do not mean the same thing. Choose the correct homonym for each blank.

creak   creek   die   dye   fir   fur

1. Did you hear that **creak** in the floor?
2. I had lunch beside the **creek** in the woods.
3. The plant will **die** without water.
4. Mother will **dye** my white pants blue.
5. A **fir** tree is always green.
6. A bear has soft brown **fur**.

flew   flu   flour   flower   new   knew

1. The birds **flew** away when we came near.
2. Kathy is feeling ill with a case of the **flu**.
3. Mother used **flour** to make the bread.
4. The pink **flower** smells so pretty!
5. I have **new** shoes.
6. Rick **knew** the answer before I did.

©1995 Kelley Wingate Publications, Inc.   98   KW 1013

Name _____ skill: homonyms

Homonyms are words that sound the same but are spelled differently and do not mean the same thing. Choose the correct homonym for each blank.

groan   grown   guessed   guest   hair   hare

1. Sue began to **groan** when she hurt her arm.
2. The children have **grown** this past year.
3. You are a **guest** in our house.
4. We **guessed** the answer right away.
5. The man has a lot of **hair** on his face.
6. Another name for a rabbit is **hare**.

hear   here   high   hi   hole   whole

1. Can you **hear** the music?
2. Put the chair right **here** on the rug, please.
3. The kite is **high** in the sky.
4. John is friendly and says **hi** to everyone he meets.
5. The rabbit jumped down into a **hole** under the bush.
6. We ate the **whole** cake!

©1995 Kelley Wingate Publications, Inc.   99   KW 1013

Answer Key

Name _____ skill: homonyms

Homonyms are words that sound the same but are spelled differently and do not mean the same thing. choose the correct homonym for each blank.

hour   our   knight   night   knot   not

1. Sixty minutes makes one **hour**.

2. That is **our** house.

3. The **knight** lived in a castle.

4. Stars come out each **night** when the sun goes down.

5. My shoelace is in a **knot** and I cannot untie it.

6. We will **not** go to the show tonight.

know   No   made   maid   mail   male

1. Do you **know** how to do this?

2. **No**, I cannot do that right now.

3. We **made** a birdhouse to hang in the tree.

4. Our **maid** cleans the house every Tuesday.

5. Please **mail** this letter for me.

6. A **male** is a boy, not a girl!

Name _____ skill: homonyms

Homonyms are words that sound the same but are spelled differently and do not mean the same thing. Choose the correct homonym for each blank.

meat   Meet   missed   mist   oar   or

1. We get our **meat** from different kinds of animals.

2. **Meet** me by the slide after school.

3. I **missed** two days of school when I was sick.

4. The low cloud made a thick **mist** over the land.

5. We row boats with a wooden **oar**.

6. I will drink either milk **or** juice with my dinner.

one   won   pail   pale   pair   pear

1. I only had **one** piece of candy today.

2. Sally **won** the race because she finished first.

3. I carried water in the green **pail**.

4. She looked **pale**, as if she had seen a ghost.

5. I have a new **pair** of purple socks.

6. We picked a **pear** from the fruit tree.

Name _____ skill: homonyms

Homonyms are words that sound the same but are spelled differently and do not mean the same thing. Pick the correct homonym for each blank.

piece   peace   peal   Peel   plain   plane

1. I want a big **piece** of cake.

2. I wish for **peace** around the world.

3. The bells will **peal** when I ring them!

4. **Peel** the apples and I will make a pie.

5. I like **plain** white milk, with nothing in it.

6. We took a **plane** to grandfather's house.

rain   reign   read   red   rose   rows

1. It looks as if it may **rain** because there are black clouds.

2. The king will **reign** for many years because he is only six years old.

3. I **read** a very good book last week.

4. Her face turned **red** because she was embarrassed.

5. Be careful of the thorns when you pick a **rose**.

6. The desks in our classroom are in neat little **rows**.

Super Reader Award

_____

receives this award for

_____

Keep up the great work!

_____   _____

signed   date

Reading Award

_____

receives this award for

_____

Great Job!

_____   _____

signed   date

Great Job!

Receives this award for

_____

Keep up the great work!

_____

Signed

Date

Great Job!

Receives this award for

_____

Keep up the great work!

_____

Signed

_____

Date

Great Job!

Receives this award for

_____

Keep up the great work!

_____
Signed

_____
Date

Congratulations!

Receives this award for

_____

Keep up the great work!

_____
Signed

_____
Date

Congratulations!

Receives this award for

_____

Keep up the great work!

_____

Signed

Date

Congratulations!

Receives this award for

_____

Keep up the great work!

_____
Signed

_____
Date

against	blanket	build	change
again	belt	brave	capture
adult	beautiful	bottom	candy
actor	allow	born	bury

clothes	climate	chief	cheese
crop	country	cold	coat
engine	elected	earth	disturb
explorer	experiment	escape	equator

found	grade	idea	islands
forest	fur	hole	invent
follow	freeze	heavy	inch
flying	freedom	hat	important

keep	kill	land	leader
legend	local	lumber	machine
main	middle	mineral	motor
mountain	mystery	newspaper	nut

ocean	orchard	outdoors	parent
people	pilot	pioneer	plane
plant	president	problem	reach
really	remember	return	ripe

same	someone	step	winner
sailed	snack	spring	touch
root	secret	spin	think
road	saw	special	strong